CW00434528

Talking to Teer

Helen Harvey

This book is dedicated to my children, who have taught me more about love and life than any book could.

Cover photo by Photo by Almos Bechtold on Unsplash

Published internationally by Helen Harvey

ABOUT ME

A bit about me and why I feel I have something to offer the world in relation to parenting teenagers and understanding them.

As well as my formal training to be a child and adolescent therapist, I have a rich canvas of experiences that I am able to tap into when parenting my children and working with children and teenagers in private practice.

I am the youngest of four with a learning delay due to a hearing impairment. I lost my father in a motor bike accident when he was 44 years old and I was 14 years old. I know about coping and resilience and in turn delayed grief.

I worked in a therapeutic community for drug and alcohol abuse and learnt that it is relational empathy that meets those unmet needs.

I have a son with additional needs, he required portage and speech and language services and eventually medication, but off all the things he really needs is to have a parent who is attuned and patient, with clear boundaries.

I have suffered anxiety, as has my daughter. It's about excepting and managing it and really being tuned in to the triggers.

I have experienced trauma and know how it can change your world view and your sense of being unsafe, causing you to become hypervigilant.

I worked in a school counselling service for 2 years as well as working in private practice for the past 4 years. I have also worked in post adoption with children who have experienced early childhood trauma.

I don't have a PhD, but I do have a wealth of emotional life and professional experience, in addition I have a successful Facebook community on my Talking to Teenagers page and I am a mumsnet blogger. I have also been ranked in the top 20 of parenting blogs by feedspot.

Enjoy the book and I welcome your comments either on my page or by email.

Helen Harvey (Dedicated Adolescent Counsellor) BA Hons, MBACP

Helenharveycounselling.com

Talkingtoteenagers@mail.com

Table of Contents

INTRODUCTION

I'm not going to go on about how hard it is to parent teenagers, you know this is the case because you have bought this book. All I want to say is that it is temporary

(Dictionary definition: lasting for only a limited period of time; not permanent)

And that it is thankless, definition: ((of a job or task) difficult or unpleasant and not likely to be satisfying or to be appreciated by others)

This books aim is to provide advice on how to attune to your teenager and not let the emotional connection widen to the point where you are both isolated and longing to connect.

I have written a little at the start of the book about self-care. People bang on about self-care all the time, it's like it's the new buzz word. I don't tend to go on about it because some parents feel it is something they just do when the time affords it. However, I have written three pieces that are important to read, to remind you that life isn't just about parenting.

When I talk in this book about being attuned to your teenager, I am talking about an experience that engages all the following things, being attuned is a way of being with your teenager that allows for an open, trusting relationship. Sometimes parents make the assumption that because they are parents that their teenager will instinctively be honest and trusting towards them. However, as the adolescent developmental tasks are underway, particularly autonomy; the teenager starts to experience her/himself as separate and see the adults in their life as more than mum and dad. They start to see an adult wrangling with their own flaws, they realise there is not a structured plan and that the parent is finding their adult way as much as the teenager is finding his adolescent way. I try to practice the following in my 'way of being' with my children. It's hard, but it is what I strive for. Also

"Don't forget to bring your funny bone along on the parenting journey, humour is a universal language that topples walls, connects hearts, and opens the door to communication and cooperation"

L.R Knost

Give and take – Meeting them half way. Hearing their stance, disagreeing with their behaviour but not the teenager.

Equality – Treating them fairly with as much emotional space as you would give yourself or your partner. Allowing them a voice.

Security – providing a sense of privacy within the relationship, I see lots of teenagers that are extremely uncomfortable with their experiences being shared to wider family members or parent's friends.

Expansive – It's a learning relationship, not just in the sense of the teenager knowing when and where they have gone wrong but learning in the sense of asking you a serious, sometimes probing question and you giving an honest informative answer.

Happy/humour – Trying to have a laugh in the face of something really difficult, especially if our teenagers are suffering from mental health issues.

Spontaneous – Whether this be spontaneity on your part or you allow room for your teenager to be spontaneous (without affecting your plans), it is healthy and teaches them, it's ok to change plans and sometimes do something good for yourself and others. Such as, I pick my daughter up from a friend and we go for a hot chocolate at the garden centre unplanned.

Courageous - This is asking tentatively about topics/behaviour you would rather not think about and try and avoid. Not be intrusive but allow the teenager to know that you are aware of something that may need a discussion to help them and then you wait patiently for that discussion to come to you.

Noticing – Probably the hardest one. Recently I wrote about really listening to your teenager's conversations or comments and noticing their verbal or non-verbal behaviour. The aim of this is to look for themes within their narrative. It is about zooming out and seeing what has changed or noticing their influences. As parents it is difficult because it needs conscious attention, but when you do it you are able to notice themes such as:

Disappointment in themselves or you as parents

Or generally betrayal, intrusion, privacy, being noticed, injustice in a system, inadequate, loss of trust etc.

These themes do not need to be fed back to your teenager but held in mind for your interactions with them.

When your teenager frequently comes to you with friendships and relationship problems, it is useful to concentrate on the teenagers input into the situation and not the situation itself.

e.g. She/he is being excluded, used, exploited, put upon, electing to be the group organiser and then feeling overwhelmed etc. It is easy to become engrossed in exploring the details of the incident/situation, but a more useful thing to do would be to explore the teenager's responsibility in this. What is the lure in this role, how does the teenager benefit. You could use the following questions to explore this

1)How do you think your input is viewed by your friends

2)How do you think it makes them feel?

3) in turn how does that make you feel?

4) What need is it meeting in you?

This helps your teenager to understand the dynamics of a situation and to explore the input of their role.

On a different note,

I don't want this book to be about what not to do, however there are a couple of things I would like to mention.

1) Nagging, you become like the dog that continually barks in the garden four doors down, sometimes you can ignore it and concentrate on something else, but sometimes it just drives you mad. The teenager can zone out from it and then of course it isn't effective or he becomes resentful and angry. They see it as a form of criticism because mum/dad mustn't trust me to do that said thing.

   Put simply, nagging just doesn't work.

2) Refresh your memory and don't shame.

   Think about some of the things you used to do as a teenager, think about the bad decisions you made and the risky behaviour. The things you did that if your parents had found out you would have been mortified.
   When I trained in cognitive behavioural therapy, I was taught that humans can't habituate to shame, meaning that no matter how much a person thinks of a shameful event, they can't lessen the distress attached to it the more they think of it. Shame is not a motivator for change, it just deepens distress and the person turns the shame in on themselves (self-harm behaviour, low self-worth, ending up in a bad situation they feel a bad person deserves)

   Expressing that you understand the behaviour but you are disappointed by it and stating how you want it to change is a message that says you can separate the behaviour from the teenager. Name calling, involving other parties unnecessarily or berating is shaming and saying that your love is conditional.

Some helpful sentences in interactions can be:

What do you think about what has happened/your behaviour/my behaviour etc.?

I hear you are unhappy about it, which bit do you want me to help you with?

I think you feel I criticize you, I don't mean to do that...what would be more helpful way of us talking?

Just some general things I do to try and show I am connected

I try and give myself 30 seconds before I respond to anything that is said from my teenager that I think is unfair.

I text my daughter at school to remind her about certain things that are school related, but also to say I love her.

One of the essential things required to help teenagers is the willingness to hear and see their distress. If you respond with *'oh, it will be alright, we can do something about that, things aren't so bad'* you are not validating their feelings. It would be more appropriate to say, 'try and explain how you feel, I notice it makes you upset, what bit is upsetting?'

This allows your teenager to feel truly heard.

SELF-CARE

The time is now – yes now, is the right time!

I love swimming, this is how it goes for me. If I don't swim, I start to feel a little overwhelmed and a little anxious. So, I have started training again and I have signed up to swim the length of Loch Earn in September and after that, maybe in 2019/2020 to swim from Spain to Morocco.

I except this is extreme, but I love swimming. I'm not a fast or brilliant swimmer by the way but I love it.

I recently had a conversation with my good friend and fellow counsellor about wish lists and goals, she has a 15-year-old and a 22-year-old. Both have been a challenge, both children have created their fair share of stress.

She simply said, "*do it because when is the right time, are you waiting for it to be easier, it might not ever be easier. Are you waiting for the kids to grow up, Helen you will be 50 then, I hope you want to swim the Gibraltar strait at 50, but there is a good chance you won't? Are you waiting to feel fitter, more on top of things, there is always going to be something and I've realised that you have to face things with courage and except they will keep coming*"

Your teenager in teenage years (and certainly younger children) are never going to say,

- *I totally see you need a break mum, so I'll stop causing aggro and be better at school*

- *I know you've always wanted to XYZ mum so I'm going to stop causing you huge amounts of stress and act like a reasonable, responsible teenager.*

- *Mum I can totally see your point of view, Joe is a bad influence because he smokes weed and acts like a div at the weekend.*

- *I know my actions cause you to have on average 5 hours sleep a night and you feel paralysed with anxiety about my future years, so I'm going to dump the 'bad news' girlfriend and study 4 hours a day.*

THIS IS NEVER GOING TO HAPPEN; YOUR TEENAGERS ARE NEVER GOING TO SAY THIS.

So, if you are waiting until you lose weight, get financially straight, be anxiety free, be separated, get the house sorted, have a better relationship with your mum, be more organised.

STOP IT!

Because you are relinquishing control, you are allowing someone to dictate your life through their actions. You are giving permission for this. If the problem relates to your teenager, you are saying to yourself that they can restrict and control your future happiness while you worry about theirs. So,

- sign up for the fun run
- go on your murder mystery weekend.
- Join the gym
- Take up running
- Join an evening class
- Book the yoga retreat
- Book the fancy restaurant
- Set up your craft business
- Apply for a different job
- Join the dating site
- buy the puppy
- Start the volunteering role

Go do, involve yourself, interact, have structure, work towards something. Do something with intention, have courage.

Because the aggro will just keep coming anyway!

If you would like to learn about worry and anxiety, I am creating a comprehensive online course for parents who's worrying is paralysing and out of control. It will involve video tutorials, worksheets, online community and ongoing support. It will be an integrative therapy approach to Generalised anxiety with a particular focus on anxiety around teenagers/children

Please email me at talkingtoteenagers@mail.com to express an interest.

Do you feel all squeezed out? Only one week to go... what parents can do to feel recharged as we go into September and the new school year.

We are on the home straight now parents. After next week, a different set of arguments will replace the ones about spending money, bus fares, lifts and how there is never anything good to eat in the house.

After the pressure of seeing to your children's needs and priorities for six weeks, you can easily find that your tank is on empty. Added to this, you may have been abroad for a sunny holiday, one that you have looked forward to since early in the year. The holiday is now past and we are entering autumn days. Some people struggle with this.

Added to all this your child may be starting secondary school this September, you will understandably have a little anxiety about this, if so please see my previous post.

https://helenharveycounselling.blogspot.com/2017/08/is-your-child-starting-secondary-school.html

The trick to self- care is that resources have to outweigh demands. Resources are biological, psychological and social.

Bio: sleep, eating, drinking, rest

Psycho: Knowledge, humour, attitude, learning, knowing boundaries

Social: friends, family, work colleague,

Demands in adults are working, family, self-expectations, friendships, money commitments, running a house etc. To clarify these demands are about topping up resources.

A very important tip is for you to be aware of your boundaries, otherwise other people will deplete the resources tank.

Here are some examples:

The friend who's a bit of a drain, who wants to moan but not change anything.

The boss at work that says '*you can do that can't you Sally, that's your speciality. Can you have it to me by Friday.*

The husband that says '*but you've said before you like doing the laundry and everything to be tidy.*

I could give you loads of examples, I'm sure you get the gist. For now, it will be just enough to notice your boundary while you fill up the resource tank.

1)   If Facebook is the first thing you look at in the morning, get rid of the people on Facebook that make you groan. Start your day of with a fighting chance. It's a platform to enhance life and connect, not suck the energy out of you.

2)   Learn that when somebody is talking about stuff that doesn't really affect you, it is ok to say "*Oh that sort of stuff doesn't bother me*" ... *really... yeah I don't care.*'

3)   Driving back from work, pick the most scenic spot, pull over and just sit for 5 mins. Notice everything outside the car, in fact get out of the car if you can. I don't just mean look around, I mean pay close attention. There are at least 144 five-minute slots in your waking day. Taking this one is no big deal.

4)   Do you have a trampoline or a sun lounger? Take the time to lie there and watch the clouds pass, this is ultra-relaxing, especially on a

trampoline (my anxious clients really say this works) It does, I know because I do it.

5)   When your rushing around, shouting at your primary school aged child "You're are going to be late", take a moment to realise that somebody somewhere decided start time was 9 o clock, society decided that. But today you are going to be a non-conformist. Today you are going to be 10 minutes late. So, what, it doesn't happen every day!

6)   Ask for help – Some people struggle with this one, especially if they have had to be very self-reliant as a child. Whether your struggle is big or small, reach out. People are willing to help with the kids, the lifts etc and if it's a bigger struggle, you need to trust that your group of friends will help and support you. If you don't trust that, it time to change friends.

7)   Check in with your emotions, sit still and figure out what your predominant feeling is:

 Anger, sadness, embarrassment, frustration, anxiety, Ashamed? You owe it to yourself to understand how you feel, so you don't walk around all churned up.

8)   Download audio books or podcasts that make you laugh, play these to and from work instead of listening to the news. It reminds you not to take life so seriously.

9)   Think about what scares you and do something towards lessening that fear. Learn something about the fear, read how other people have worked towards overcoming it. Educate yourself. Know everything there is to know about that fear and why it triggers you. While doing this have a cup of tea and some chocolate chip cookies on hand. If it's an emotional life experience, connect with similar people on forums and

Facebook groups. If it requires it, get some professional help – that IS looking after yourself.

10) Spend more time in nature and get more sleep, both are a basic need and just as important as each other. FOR EVERY LOST HOUR OF SLEEP THERE IS A 38% INCREASE IN FEELINGS OF SADNESS AND HOPELESSNESS.

The government last year supported the 3 main green care interventions for improved mental health suggested by Nature England, care farming, environmental conservation and social and therapeutic horticulture. Being outside is therapeutic!

With the waves slapping in my mouth and up my nose... I heard the helicopter and thought it had come for me!... Setting your own challenge as a parent, what do you and your children gain?

I am 41 and my mum is the most supportive person I know, positive with my children, positive attitude in work, resilient and wise. The one thing my mum is a little of, is risk averse. There are many reasons for this, one being, living with my dad, her husband, who regularly did risky things that didn't pay off.

Last year I announced to her that I was going to swim the Solent in aid of the Ian Pratt MND foundation. I casually said *'you know, swim from mainland to the Isle of Wight, hundreds of people have done it'*. Hundreds of people haven't done it in fact, but I decided to lie a bit to get her on board. She said

'I'm worried, it's dangerous' when that didn't seem to have an impact; she said *'is it not a little irresponsible, you've got a husband and two children'*

Driving these not so helpful responses was anxiety and love. As parents when we predict an outcome or share our worry, we are saying I can't sit, feel and tolerate the anxiety. Don't get me wrong, my mum has done her fair share of tolerating anxiety (she has 4 strong willed children), but she was asking me not to invite anxiety unnecessarily. After her initial worry, she understood and became very supportive about the swim.

So, when you have a teenager that is creating anxiety and worry in you, it is hard to decide to challenge yourself, do something risky and grow from it, because it feels like you have no more room for anxiety of your own.

Nearly everybody has heard reference to the comfort zone, there are lots of inspirational people speaking inspirational quotes about personal growth. What are the central messages in these quotes? Challenge and determination wins the day and changes you. None of these quotes say *'yes you feel scared sh**less and your waking at 3am with your heart pounding out your chest but forget all that. Just do it'.*

What I'm going to explain in this blog, is that when that is happening, the exact thing to do is to embark on a challenge of your own. Here is why.

·   Because it gives you a sense of the bigger picture; loosing perspective is easy as a parent and our friends want to seem empathetic and supportive so they say things like *'no wonder your worried, I would be'* and it might be something big to worry about, but worry isn't action and it rarely provides answers as it is coming from the amygdala, which is the emotional part of the brain.

·   Setting up a challenge is acknowledging to yourself and to other family members that you have a need as important as all their needs.

Yes, you are a parent, but you are allowed a life and to be passionate about things.

·   When you have signed up for something, you are forced to dedicate the right amount of time to it. This is a good thing, it gives you timeout, a different focus, an interest to read about and learn.

·   It gives you another aspect of identity, not just a parent but a mature student maybe, triathlete, reading club coordinator, swimmer.

Now if you will allow and read on, I would like to tell you about my challenge; which will explain the title of this blog and you will learn what lessons I took from it.

5am start, I wake my nine-year-old, I wake my husband (bags already packed) and we start on the road, 300 miles down to Portsmouth.

My safety briefing is at 1pm and my swim starts at 2pm. I have raised nearly £1600 and trained in a disused quarry that is a dive centre for about 9 months. Sometimes I have swum in water as low as 6 degrees. What has this taught me? That my body can endure short bursts of very cold water and that water invigorates me.

What has my training taught me? That with some improvements and hard work, I am as capable as any other swimmer to complete this swim. Ceri, my trainer trusts me to put the work in and tunes into my need to succeed. She teaches me that there is no short cut or easy way.

Prior to my swim I researched about Motor Neurone Disease and the Ian Pratt foundation and have learnt that life expectancy of people diagnosed with MND is on average between 3 to 5 years, around half will die within 14 months. MND kills around 5 People every day in the UK. Ian Pratt who was diagnosed in 2012 wants to raise awareness that this disease will eventually deprive him of the ability to walk, to move, to talk, to eat and breathe. His foundation funds support, awareness and research. To learn more about the terrific work they do go to https://www.facebook.com/IanPrattMNDF/ or

http://www.swimmingthesolent4mnd.com/contact-us/

We arrive and go through the safety briefing. The Solent is a strait that separates the Isle of Wight from main land England and is a major shipping lane for military, passenger and freight vessels. Every swimmer has a safety Kayaker and there are two safety motor boats for everyone, just in case. The distance we need to swim is 2.5 miles, but with currents you can end up swimming close to 3. Safety is the priority, we talk about procedures for when we struggle during swimming.

We are given Ian Pratt MND wristbands to take over the Solent. Those wristbands are sent to people all across the world who have lost a loved one to Motor Neurone Disease.

I stand on the beach in my wetsuit, thermal hat, gloves and boots. I could be in the water for over two and a half hours. I don't want to get cold. I have specially made moulded earplugs and a tight rubber cap over my first thermal cap, hearing is limited, not the best idea.

The wind is picking up a little; I kiss my son and husband and get in the water. Zippy and Paul, my Kayakers have spoken to me, telling me to keep close, but a safe distance as not to collide. Zippy has swam the Solent, I am in safe hands.

I start swimming, I'm terrified.

I realise my training bears no relevance to the task I need to complete. I feel in trouble and I keep stopping. I keep trying but get a mouth full of water every time a wave comes. All I think is "I have another 2 hours of this". Zippy shouts that '*it will get better when we get past the big metal buoy*,' she shouts it again, she is smiling and is optimistic and encouraging.

This moment is probably the most important in all the swim, what did it teach me? It taught me that you guess your own limitations when rational thinking shuts off when scared or worried, but here was a person seeing me differently. Zippy didn't know my thinking, she didn't see those limitations. She was saying its ok, I've felt that and I get it, but let's press on.

Later I learnt that my son started to cry on the beach at that moment, because he could see that I was struggling. My husband reassured him that the whole event was surrounded by safety measures and that the worst thing that could happen was that I didn't complete the swim, but no harm was going to come to me.

I swapped sides with the kayak and got into a rhythm. It felt like I was managing, I was getting used to the task. Maybe just over a mile in, a second kayak came to sandwich me in and ensure my direction was right. The sea was a bit choppy with swells. The current was so strong that it was pulling us east. I could hear a helicopter overhead. I turned and said to the new kayaker *'that helicopter isn't for me, is it'* he laughed and shouted *'no if that helicopter was for you, my face would look a lot more worried than it does now'*

I was disappointed with the need for a second kayaker, but later I have learnt that my helpers were giving me the best possible chance of completing the swim in the correct place.

We pressed on, all the time these people believing that I could complete this swim. The current was so strong that it was decided we would abandon our planned landing point near the pier and instead come in on the sands about half a mile east.

Just over the half way point I got stuck in a current, I was swimming and swimming and not moving, a decision was made to move me sideways, I panicked and said *'I've got to do the full distance'*, the guy on the boat shouted back *'you are still doing the distance, we aren't moving you any further in across the swim, just sideways'*

The sensation of sea swimming when you are out in the middle is a little like being in a washing machine on a gentle hand wash wool cycle, the motion is never ending, sometimes gentle swaying, but often, steady solid rocking. I began to feel seasick so I started to sing the songs my sister and I had chosen exactly for this purpose. Stand by Me is a great song and even more poignant in this task.

I don't know how much further it was after that point, my sensory deficit with ear plugs and fogged up goggles obscured my distance gauging abilities. What I do know is that I have never been happier to see sand beneath the water on my way in.

My husband and son waded out to greet me, my son said

'you've done it, I'm so proud' I started to cry and replied

'I struggled it was really hard'

My son replied *'YEAH BUT YOU DID IT'*

What a fantastic life lesson to watch and digest as a nine year and a fourteen-year-old.

So, what have I learnt and gained from this challenge?

·   That other people can see your potential and if you allow yourself, you can trust those people and learn something about your capabilities.

·   That even in the worst time when I was scared, my commitment became unwavering because these people believed in me as did my family and friends.

· That as a parent, you need something else to push you through and work towards. To explore, work on and develop that other aspect of you that has nothing to do with parenting.

· I feel emotionally stronger and a little changed in some way. I set a goal, I worked towards that goal when things got in the way. I felt fearful, but I achieved, and that makes my heart feel bigger.

GOSH WHAT IS IT WITH TEENAGERS?

How we feel about self-harm, effects how we respond.

One of the issues I work with frequently with teenagers is self-harm. Self-harm can feel complex and overwhelming to parents and school staff who see it as a destructive behaviour. It is extremely distressing for the young person and also for the parent that feel powerless to stop it.

It is destructive in its nature but is also a coping strategy to regulate feelings that feel powerful and overwhelming. When I worked in a school counselling team, school staff used to describe it as attention seeking, but in fact it is attention needing. What do I mean by this?

The teenager is trying to understand and regulate these difficult emotions and is seeking to connect. What self-harm provides is a frequent return to a regulated state that the person has ultimate control over.

Many young people report that it feels like a release of tension and agitation, that the tension release is freeing. In counselling and other arenas such as a supportive conversation at home, the teenager needs to work towards recognising and managing distressing feelings. First, they would need to identify the triggers to these feelings and work towards finding more functional ways of regulating them. This could be through dance, exercise, expressive drawing etc. This requires some flexibility from you and your teenager to try out things they wouldn't ordinarily consider.

Depressed teenagers feel a sense of numbness to the world. They feel detached and disconnected. It's like the window screen of life has a thin layer of fog, keeping the teenager from feeling alive. In these client's self-harm serves to help the teenager feel quickened and restored. Temporarily they feel connected again. I feel it's a bit like an electric shock that brings them back to life. Activities that give the same sensation such as cold-water swimming would help in this instance.

Another reason for self-harm could be a way to care for themselves and elicit care from Adults in their life. When they care for cuts and bruises it is an opportunity to be caring towards themselves. To give themselves love and kindness and for other people to show this to them as well. In these cases, young people could start to understand that they deserve care and attention without the self-harm. As a parent you could really concentrate on finding ways where the young person can physically care for themselves. Such as skin care routine, massage,

Tumblr have lots of suggestions and pointers on self-harm and self-care.

The other more concerning reason young people self-harm is that they do it to punish themselves. This is sometimes because they hold very high expectations for themselves and believe they haven't met theirs or somebody else's expectations or they believe they deserve to be punished. Some young people I have worked with believe they are inherently bad and bad people need punishment. It is a longer more complex therapeutic process, but work involving self-esteem, challenging negative thoughts, being truly heard, can work towards a more positive sense of self.

This book: The Self-Esteem Workbook for Teens: Activities to Help You Build Confidence and Achieve Your Goals. Can help with self-esteem.

If the young person is conscious of the scars once they have healed, then bio oil helps a lot with lightening the colour and healing the skin.

It remains still a mystery why some people continue to self-harm and continue to do it into adulthood, when some people lose this behaviour in late adolescence even when therapy has been provided. The important thing is to keep the communication lines open and to try and not show your own distress to the young person as this perpetuates the young person's guilty feelings.

*A salute to j17 magazine, the
engaged ringtone and Constance
Carroll lipstick. How much harder
is it to be a teenager nowadays?*

What were the media influences we relied upon as teenagers to navigate the world of fashion, culture and friendship in the 80's? They were magazines with proper editors who made the final decision on appropriateness and topical content. It was Jeff Banks on the clothes show telling you what was "in fashion" or as they say now 'on point'

It was Grange Hill showing you the valuable lessons in friendships, World in Action making you aware of the bigger injustices worldwide and John Craven delivering the news in the kindest child friendly way on Newsround. Our media influences were funnelled and filtered to ensure the content matched the audience.

How did we know Constance Carroll Heather shimmer lipstick was all the rage? j17 told us. How did you know if your friend was in to chat with, the phone was engaged, then you biked yourself round and stayed until just before crossroads finished and biked back.

 The point I am trying to make is that living in that era gave us a certainty and predictability about what we should tune into, the options were limited. Today's version is an onslaught of life lessons from the Kardashian's and Love Island, that we choose to allow are teenagers to buy into.

I thought the other day that I should just open my front door and allow any waif and stray to walk up to my daughter's bedroom and form an orderly que so they can fill her brain with all sorts of useless and damaging things that will change her world view; give comparisons that she'd never given thought to before and to top it off, be given enough of everybody's drama to put Eldorado to shame.

No, don't bother with that. The iPhone is doing the job for me.

Adolescence is now a very different landscape, the internet influences how they spend their time, how they behave and their attitude towards sexuality, socializing, school and expected lifestyle. Not only is the internet piping crap into our teenager's brain and teaching them things they didn't care to learn about before, but social media use and screen time generally is hiking up the statistics on loneliness.

Loneliness in teens had been generally trending downwards until 2012, then it started to rise and kept rising until in 2014 it reached an all-time high. So... now we don't just have to worry about the epidemic of loneliness amongst elderly through no fault of their own, no... now we need to worry about the loneliness of our teenagers, who are on social media to feel included...Oh the irony!

Teenagers are spending more leisure time alone, they are communicating by snapchatting, texting and Instagram.

The results of recent research are clear: 14-year old's who spend more than 10 hours a week on social media are 56% more likely to be unhappy than the teens that don't. If they spend six hours a day on social media they are still 47% more likely to say they are unhappy (Twenge, 2017)

So, our teenagers only have to be on social media 50 minutes a day to feel unhappy.

How was it for us? when you finished reading Just 17 magazine you went and did something else. When you finished recording the top 40 onto your cassette you occupied yourself in another way. Same after Top of the Tops. These things have stop cues, meaning the activity comes to a natural end and you are forced to do something else. The trouble with social media, including YouTube, which now automatically loads another video, as does Facebook, is that you can consume huge amounts of irrelevant crap. Before you know it 90 minutes has gone.

Every element of teenager's life now has a level of intensity that would be difficult to replicate in any other era. GCSE pressure is in one of these areas. I have written about the topic of school stress and what you can do to help here
https://helenharveycounselling.blogspot.com/2017/08/do-you-have-child-doing-their-gcses.html

What do teenagers need to be afraid off, the terrorists or Brexit, the on-street groomers or the illegal highs? The fact that before they have even sat an exam, they get told that 600 people are applying for any job they ever apply for. But that's ok because they are going to be youtubers or vloggers instead because it's obvious that any moron can jump around in front of a camera and play tricks on their brother and get paid ££££'s for it in advertising. "it's not that easy" you say and your teenager looks at you like you have two heads and you're the deluded one.

In the summer my teenage daughter showed me a peers Instagram page and asked me to agree it was 'edgy' One of the photos was a picture of a hotel sink with filters. I replied "*it's a sink*" my daughter agreed that she could see that, but it was an "edgy photo" "*and you are admired if you have an edgy Instagram account*" Ok brilliant, so the reality is it's not about posting photos of memories you have created and experiences you have enjoyed, or at the very worst what you have purchased and want to brag about. No, now you are judged on your artistic perception and interpretation...hold on, wait there while I go and take an arty photo of my knackered broken bird table.

I'm joking a little about a very serious situation. It's worth noting that the giants of the tech industry limit their children's interaction on devices. The late Steve Jobs stated that his kids had not used the iPad and that they actively limited the amount of tech their children were allowed to use at home.

I believe that if we can't change the context of these social media platforms then we should limit it like anything that is bad for us. Everything in moderation. Sometimes our teenagers need to be shown what moderation looks like. I'm going to suggest to my daughter 20 mins after school, 20 minutes after tea and 10 minutes before bed. When my daughter gave up Snapchat in May this year (she hasn't been back on it) she started to spend time alongside me doing art projects and teaching me card games. This facilitated other discussions that were important and we were able to be more attuned.

Do you want to know what one of the leading psychologists think we should do about the ever-increasing epidemic of poor teenage mental health? Steven Biddulph believes as parents we should stop acting like we have no control over it and parent the situation with firm warm boundaries. His suggestion is no screen time in bedrooms and more time spent in the company of your teenagers. He believes that a 5%

change in the way parents operate could be enough to shift your daughter out of the mental health zone.

I don't know what he means by the term 'operate', but if he means more time spent together in an attuned way, then I think that leaves us responsible to be relaxed and accepting about what your teenager brings. This is not an easy task, getting the balance right between interested but not intrusive is a daily guessing game.

It is no coincidence that statistics regarding teenagers and unhappiness started to be significant when the use of social media platforms increased in teenagers. Maybe this is a call to action.

Bring back the Just 17 era, but maybe not the Constance Carroll lipstick.

References

iGen: Why Today's Super-Connected Kids Are Growing Up Less Rebellious, More Tolerant, Less Happy--and Completely Unprepared for Adulthood--and What That Means for the Rest of Us

https://www.thetimes.co.uk/article/parenting-how-to-help-girls-grow-up-happy-kp5fb2wcf

What's going on in the teenager
brain, why it's important for
parents to understand!

What's going on with the teenage brain, one minute your teenager is laughing and chatting on the phone, then you ask a simple question and his mood explodes like a party popper all over the house (only it doesn't feel like a party) and you feel like you have been on the receiving end of something really unfair. The dictionary example of unfair is *not following the rules of a game or sport*, the Cambridge dictionary example is *not treating people in an equal way or not morally right*. Both of these examples are true for parents of teenagers, you or I wouldn't put it in these terms, but the essence of the feeling is in these statements.

So, what is going on?

Imagine your teenagers brain as a tree and just before puberty there is an increase in grey matter in the prefrontal cortex, this part of the brain is responsible for logic and reasoning which helps with decision making. Unfortunately, during adolescence, the tree is pruned and cut back to generate stronger and sturdier branches in late adolescence (18 years ish). During adolescence your teenager will lose about 15% of grey matter resulting in less logical thinking, risky behaviours, reduced ability to stay on task etc.

So what part of the brain is driving so much obnoxious behaviour?

It's a part of the brain that is emotional, highly reactive, impulsive. This part is called the amygdala and is thousands and thousands of years old.

During brain scans of adolescents this part seemed to be working feverishly when shown a picture and asked to describe a facial expression. The facial picture was fear, but the adolescents answered variedly. anger, shock, disgust and pain were some of the answers.

Next time there is an emotional explosion in your house and you wonder what caused the break in communication, some of the answer is the AMYGDALA. It helps to keep this in mind, because we can react to these explosions too easily. We can take things personally when actually there is a totally different reason for behaviour than your teenager wanting to hurt or anger you.

When your children were young and ill with chicken pox or something similar and they were grouchy and teary and hard work, you were able to say '*it's understandable they are ill*'

You can sometimes do this now in teenage years and instead say '*it's understandable, her/his brain is under construction*'.

DON'T GET ME WRONG IT ISNT OK FOR BAD BEHAVIOUR, BUT IT IS SOMETHING TO HOLD IN MIND WHEN DISHING OUT THE CONSEQUENCES.

More to come on teenage behaviour and how to manage it.

<u>Let's talk about sleep, teenagers and anxiety...the statistics are unsettling!!</u>

Sleep (or lack of it) is one of the biggest contributors to poor mental health. Sleep aids teenagers learning in the waking hours, memory consolidation and aids emotional processing. At the current time teenagers in this country are experiencing a sleep deprivation epidemic. Does that sound dramatic, well I assure you it is true.

1 in 10 teenagers get the 8-10 hours of sleep recommended by researchers and paediatricians. One of the reasons for this is that during puberty there is a shift in melatonin production (the hormone in your body that makes you yawn and stretch and generally feel sleepy) In teenagers this hormone is active later in the evening, around 11pm ish, but with after school activities, school work and the social media activity teenagers need to fit in, 11pm seems early. So, they fight this melatonin production, and the system becomes disrupted.

The end result is a teenager that can't think straight, who is irritable and feels terrible and they need to make it through the school day. Increasingly for some teenagers their 'go to' thing is caffeine drinks, consuming huge amounts in a day. So, then they are a teenager who is hyper and wiped out at the same time.

As I talked about in my previous post, there is huge dramatic brain development happening around this time, that sleep contributes to. It's the part of the brain that exercises good judgement and eventually will counteract the stupid risky behaviours in teenagers that are terrifying to parents.

The effects of lack of sleep go way beyond the classroom, research shows it contributes to substance use, anxiety and depression.

The statistics:

A teenager who lacks a good amount of sleep is 55% more likely to have used alcohol in the last month.

For each hour of lost sleep there is a 38% increase in feelings of sadness and hopelessness.

For teenagers with a driving license, 5 hours or less of sleep a night is the equivalent of driving with a blood alcohol level 1.5 times above the legal limit.

I am in no way the expert on sleep, but I wanted to raise the awareness around this as a contributing factor to poor mental health, in particular anxiety, as the fight or flight system is so much more activated when we have had poor sleep.

What a change and a joy it would be for teenagers and the family to experience a little less moodiness, but also for the teenager to feel revitalised and fully resourced for the day ahead.

Next post: How to aid sleep and do practical things that reduce your anxiety.

Statistics and info from sleep researcher Wendy Troxel.

*The first thing, you can do right
now to improve your relationship
with your teenager (especially if
your teenager is a boy)*

"Before you were conceived, I wanted you. Before you were born, I loved you, before you were a minute old, I would have died for you. This is the miracle of life."

Maureen Hawkins

The above statement is hard to hold onto...yes? Right now, you may be convinced that your teenager really wants to be as far away from you as possible, he takes every opportunity to be with his friends, when he is at home he is in his room, when he's in the car he is looking away out the window not talking.

So, it becomes hard to hold onto the fact that your teenager wants you in his life in some way, he needs his friends yes, but he knows that he needs his parents for support and guidance. Your teenager wants you to attentively care for him...in a non-intrusive way.

Every teenager's developmental tasks are identity, autonomy and belonging. These tasks are happening every day of the teenager's life.

The teenager's bedroom represents some aspects of this. Posters on the wall, choice of decoration, objects kept from childhood, the rules drawn up for parent's entry, safe haven etc.

My teenage clients tell me that one of the feelings that they experience the most is intrusion from a parent, boys more so. The bedroom is a physical place that symbolises this.

So, the first step towards shifting your relationship with your teenager to a better place, may be to state (in the calm moments when the lines of communication are open) that you no longer want to go in his bedroom and you recognise that this is his space and you respect that. All you ask is that he keeps it reasonably smell free. Explain that you will need to come in to wake him as the 5 alarm alerts on his phone don't work, but other than that it is his space. You can also explain that it saves you a job, you now have one less room to clean. Win - win situation. Tell him you are doing this in the hope it makes your relationship better in the long run, because that is important to you.

Also, his dirty clothes will need to be left on the landing for washing.

I know you're thinking dirty plates and cups, but when you no longer have enough of these in the kitchen to use, you can simply call up to the teenager and tell him about the shortage of crockery. Ask nicely for his cooperation in exchange for yours.

I know, I know I'm talking about all of this like it will go smoothly, I admit that in the first three weeks it won't.

However, there will be a shift in the relationship, if in the past you went into his room uninvited (even if you knocked) it will have been experienced as an intrusion. If you are quite an anxious parent, this may have come across even more because your teenager will experience you as anxious and maybe empathise with this at first, but eventually can't carry your anxiety whilst trying to progress in his developmental tasks as well.

You may be thinking that if you don't go into his room you would hardly see him and this is true, but I am speaking from experience that going in the room whilst he is relaxing isn't going to produce much attuned conversation. What happens is that we go around picking up cups and plates whilst asking questions that he doesn't want to answer; an argument happens which is carried through to the car journey. He grunts goodbye, slams the door and you are left feeling flat for the rest of the day or evening.

If you skipped the Spanish inquisition in the bedroom, there is a chance the car journey conversation would have been quite bearable (by teenage standards).

I am not condoning soft, where your teenager is allowed to stomp about and speak to everyone like crap, I am advising less contact of the intrusive sought for no reason other than to alleviate our anxiety.

The bedroom conversation is the starting point.

*Advising all Parents don't do b******t, teenagers are experts at detecting it in adults!*

Teenagers need repeated instructions, reminders, prompting, guidance and direction but when it comes to insight and awareness into the adults in their life, they are watching and tracking carefully.

Between the ages of 11-13 teenagers start to experience their parents as people that haven't quite got it together in a way they expect adult life to be. In some cases, this creates a sceptical disheartened teenager who is looking for evidence of safety and security in this 'scales fall from the eyes' period.

So, what are we to do as parents to prevent these feelings in your teenagers to deepen.

Stop the b******t

- Don't try to wing a mistake and continue to protest it was the right course of action. The teenager knows you have got it a bit wrong, they feel it. If it goes unacknowledged it becomes the elephant in the room. It's better to say 'I thought it was right at the time, I made a mistake and I got it wrong'

Because if we don't do this we teach our teenagers that a defensive stance gets us through, that we can't be open and admit when we were wrong and when the time comes in their adult relationships they can't admit they were wrong.

If you make a mistake, admit it, attempt at cover up makes your teenagers believe you are acting in bad faith.

- Use praise when you really feel pleased or surprised that they have remembered something or thought about somebody's else's point of view. When you don't have the feeling that goes along with the praise it sounds empty and false and teenagers don't feel it as true. My clients often say "Mum/Dad said XYZ, but I could tell they didn't really feel that way.

- When there is anything happening that is affecting the equilibrium of the family, tell them what's happening. Not every gritty detail, but be straight about the basics, as a lot of my clients talk about being kept in the dark and not being told what is going on and they feel aggrieved by this when the practical aspects of the situation affect them.

This is very important... what they don't know they make up and the made-up version is usually 4 times worse than what is actually going on. Better to be able to tell the truth and be in a position to reassure them, than the teenager to be alone in their head.

- Don't manipulate your teenager. Manipulation is b******t, rewards and consequences (which I have spoken about before) are not manipulation as it is a straight exchange. Manipulation is guilt tripping by sulking, whining, complaining. It is b******t because it is not a true and genuine communication.

- Don't pretend to still be mad at them, you are denying your teenager the option to digest the feelings of disappointment and to learn the lesson, some things can be over egged. Say your piece, check their understanding and then put the consequences in. I worked with one client who admitted that her mum kept it going for that long that the lesson was lost and she was just preoccupied with how to be 'friends' again.

The single biggest drive we have is to connect, it's a survival, evolutionary thing. When we detect a connection that isn't true, it feels wrong and unsettling, causing us to mistrust and ultimately disconnect.

Morning routine

Ok Parents of teenagers, let's get this morning routine whipped into shape! 5 things that you should do to make things go just a little smoother.

(doesn't include meditating)

There are certain things I did last year in the morning that made me feel like I was on the back foot. No matter how hard I tried to get ahead of the game in the morning, it just didn't come together.

This year is going to be different and it starts this week with the return to school days...hurrah!!

So tomorrow I am going to be a housekeeping ninja without having to live in the kitchen and laundry room.

1) You set your alarm for the same time every morning whether you work part time or full. It doesn't matter why or what time you got to bed the night before. You can promise yourself an early night when you get up at 7.00am

2) It is easy to stay in our PJ's, but you are not on your game in your PJ's, this stuff is all psychological. Turn the shower on and while you wait for it too warm up you can have a 5-minute scroll through Facebook if you must. Shower and dressed, if dressing is a nightmare you set a date and time (20 minutes) to sort the wardrobe situation out.

3) Before your teenager's grunt that they need breakfast. You put a load of washing in, on that 30 minutes cycle (this is an adequate cycle unless your kids do dirt biking every weekend)

4) Empty the dishwasher while you shout your too do list into that echo/Alexa thing. Or simpler version, ask your 7,8, 10, 12-year-old to write it down as you say it out loud. Tell them they have been promoted to that position and because of this they get an extra £1 at the weekend (it's worth it!)

5) Think about tea, sometimes I get carried away with fancy dinners/tea. All you have to do is think about it not prepare it. I mean something like, Jacket Potatoes with Tuna and sweetcorn, beans on toast, cheese on toast with curly fries, one of those family tray lasagne things, omelette. Yes, these seem like snacks, but add a little salad, coleslaw, garlic bread and they are a meal when you have not been prepared or done a shop. No teenager ever died because they didn't have Jamie Oliver's beef bourguignon in their weekly meal planner.

Don't get me wrong these things will not make you a rested, stress free super mum, but they may just bring some order to that time of day that sets the tone and mood for the whole family and their day.

Getting them out of bed

So, we are back to routine, are you screaming for your teenager to get out of bed yet?

Well you know that you're not on your own with this, parents of my clients complain about this regularly.

As adults we find it hard to get out of bed, but the bills and the mortgage payments and the boss gives us the motivation to get up. What does the teenager have hanging over him to make him get up on time and conquer the day...?

His assignment on music production for modern theatre, no he's got that covered because he believes he can get the guidelines emailed to him instead of attending first period/lesson. Also, Lucy who sits next to him said she can help out with that!

The fact that he will be marked down as late on his attendance record...no he's just going to come up with some doctor's appointment, bus broke down routine, he's got that covered.

The fact that mum will be totally p****d off with him and she will do that silent, only answer in curt sentences thing and tell everybody how much she does for everyone else. He's thought about that and he'll offer to take the dog out and tell her tea was really tasty.

The knowledge that if he doesn't get himself in gear and work really hard that, he will be bottom of the heap in terms of job prospects...

Of course not, that would require your teenage son or daughter to consider consequences and think long term. Something that brain science in adolescence says is very unlikely to happen as they live in the emotional part of the brain.

So, what can we do to make this situation better?

- When your teenager is in a good mood, ask him/her what would help to get them out of bed in the morning.

- Allow them to sleep in at the weekends to catch up on their sleep, but only 2 hours more on Saturday and 2 hours more on Sunday. Naps in the afternoon are going to disrupt sleep at night. If they insist on a nap in the afternoon, it's probably best to limit it to 40 minutes.

- Cut down on the caffeine, this effects sleep up to five hours after drinking concentrated doses of caffeine.

- Remove the phone at 11.00am, if they insist they need it for music to get to sleep. Give them a radio alarm clock. Inform them that this is the old-fashioned version of streaming, on demand music and a chance to broaden their musical taste.

- Get up half an hour earlier and put bacon or sausage in the grill for a sandwich, the smell and the thought of nice food might encourage them to rise.

Think about how much it means to you, for your teenager to be up and ready to leave the house on time. If him being late disrupts your commitments then you could consider financial incentives (yes, its bribing) but re read the start of this blog, your teenager is two steps ahead.

Avoid the arguing about getting up and ready, this contributes to the over blown generalized view that you are always getting at them. Keep in mind that this stage will pass, just like all the other stages, it's just adolescence lasts longer than the others.

When was it that we agreed to buy

the Adidas and pay their mobile
bill...without expecting
cooperation.

Appropriate for this time of year, when requests are frequent but a helping attitude is not.

Back in the summer, a friend explained that they were trying to get a break down south at their parents with their two children, one 9 and one 14. The 14-year-old was refusing to go. My friend was asking ' *what am I meant to do, physically man handle him into the car?'*

I looked over at the teenager son riding a £190 scooter with Nike trainers and Adidas tracksuit, talking on his iPhone 6 and said to myself "THIS IS ALL THE WRONG WAY AROUND"

When did we start to feel so disempowered in the investment/return arrangement of our children?

The teenager version of adult life looks like this. You leave for work 5 minutes before your meant to arrive there, you arrive and sit at your desk with your arms folded and your head on the desk. Every now and again you grunt an answer at someone who has interrupted you, making you remove your earphones. You go to the coffee machine in the hall and make a conscious effort to disagree with everything everyone says in a loud and obnoxious manner; you spread your stuff over other people's work surface and when they complain, you insist the problem is theirs because they require everywhere to be so tidy.

You do little work, because someone is posting funny stuff from the Lad Bible on Facebook. Your generally unpleasant to be around as you are the absolute expert on everything in the whole of the universe, but nobody wants to point this out because it zaps their energy to think about trying to put their opinion across.

Lunchtime comes and its always been an hour for lunch but you decide that isn't long enough, so you come back from lunch 20 minutes late with a blank look on your face and when the others stare, you shout 'God its only 20 minutes, chill out'

Afternoon break comes and the boss passes you in the corridor and checks you have understood the brief for Friday and enquires as to your preparations, you roll your eyes and with a defensive stance make him feel he is completely overstepping the mark by asking anything of you. He backs down and says he will check in with you at the end of the day. You stomp off muttering loudly that it's an oppressive regime.

The boss checks in with you at the end of the day, it's 5.02pm the official finish is 5.00pm and you make a point of saying he is lucky that you are still there. He asks about the costings you promised to do... by today and you say *'There just hasn't been the time, I did collect some water cups for the water dispenser though, they were right at the back of the cupboard, so really I've done my bit and can I just ask about the Christmas bonus and I need to upgrade my work phone to an iPhone X*

You wouldn't get away with it would you? But lately my teenager has been getting away with the teenage equivalent in my house, and quite frankly it's exhausting and irritating in equal measure. If somebody had said to you that this bundle of joy would grow up to ensure that you go to work just to pay the bills and buy crap that is more important than your crap and then they're going to make life as miserable as they possibly can between your age of 35-60, you would surely say...umm no thanks.

It is true that being a teenager has never been so hard, but that doesn't mean we let them off the hook with the things that really matter. Yes, they can have the expensive crap they want, but they have to fit in around family members and try. Relationships are a two-way thing, working for a business is a two-way thing. They cannot expect the trappings of a good life and not follow the rules.

Obviously, I have to do the basics, school bus pass, lunch money, clothes, food etc. Do I have to buy the Converse and the MAC makeup when my daughter is being obnoxious and not following the rules...no I don't.

This is how I dealt with it last week.

- I considered what the problem was
- I made an appointment to talk to her, *"tomorrow night I want to see you to chat at 6 o clock, please make sure your free"*
- I then stated what the behaviour was. The occasions the behaviour had been repeated (your teenager cannot then say *oh come on, what... once!*)
- I then pointed out the affect it has on everybody else. So, the outcome for others

B Behaviour

R repeats of behaviour

O outcome for others

- I then empathized that its hard being a teenager etc.
- And then we made an agreement where some of the privileges were removed until things improved and all family members felt other family members were being helpful.

I got a rolling of the eyes and a promise to try harder, an agreement to meet me a $1/3^{rd}$ of the way (half was being optimistic)

When I was a teenager I was expected to set the table, help stack the dishwasher, not swear at my siblings and not try and continue lying when the game was up. I really didn't want to do all these things, I wanted to sit in my bedroom and listen to music while not doing my homework, but if I didn't do these tasks I didn't get the rewards.

So, I do not want to put up with my teenager sulking and stomping about when I am cramming in school productions, present buying, Christmas decorating, work, laundry, taxing and work's Christmas do.

In fact, I don't want to put up with it at any time, when I'm working hard to pay the mortgage and live a little, while they believe they run the show.

Yes, I can be attuned to her and support her, but I can't let her off the hook. Because if I let her off the hook, I am setting her up to fail when she's required to deliver on the things she gets paid for.

Calling all mums, do you feel like you're the referee in your house?

You know the scenario; your daughter has left her dirty plates stacked up at the sink. Your son is 10 minutes late home. Dad/step dad wants to leave the house on time and teenage daughter is taking more than the imagined 10 minutes to get ready to join dad for the lift.

Dad tries to deal with it, but he's a bit bad tempered and short on patience so he reacts like something from a 1970's parenting manual. Teenager mutters something and before you know it, you two are arguing and teenager has gone upstairs, out the way listening to headphones on iPhone oblivious to frayed tempers and accusations of bad parenting.

Dad/other parent: "you know what the problem is don't you, your soft, that is why her bedroom looks like it does and she speaks to me in that s****y way.

Mum: "no she speaks to you in that s****y way because you are always on at her"

Dad/other parent: "what, because I ask her to clean her plates away, what a joke"

And so, it goes on.

This can be soul destroying for mums, who can't quite convey to their husband/partner what it is they offer to the teenager that brings a different result than theirs. It is true that mums do lose their temper as well, but they do something different in the more quieter moments.

My teenage clients report that mums tune in, they also report they do have meaningful conversations with dad, just less often than mum.

So, because of this, mum becomes the referee. The referee between dad/partner/stepdad and teenager, the referee between siblings etc. This over time starts to have an effect on a partnership.

How can this be prevented?

1)   In your quieter moments, agree that the arguments usually are over parenting and that the partnership overall is healthy (only if it is healthy obviously)

2)   Have a code word that you can say that indicates to you both that this is purely about different parenting styles, these differences need a discussion afterwards.

3)   Try and arrange that dad spends time with the teenager on his own (it doesn't matter what the activity is, it's about open discussion away from the home)

4)   Both parents need to remember that they were not saints as teenagers and even if they were brought up in a strict household, they probably resented this and felt misunderstood.

5)   An obvious one... do stuff without the teenagers/children, even if its buying a bag of chips and going for a walk.

6)   Have family meetings where everyone gets 7 minutes each to put their point across without anybody butting in. Everyone should try to stick to 'when you do this, I feel like this' instead of 'YOU make me feel like this'

7)   Remember that this stage will pass and that looking after yourself is needed more in this stage than some of the others. Even if this is allowing yourself to listen to music or read fiction, this is nurturing in itself.

I wish I had other suggestions, but parenting differences are difficult at any age, but parenting a teenager who 'has the answers' and rolls their eyes at the slightest annoyance is difficult not to comment on.

Maybe it's about widening our window of patience.

My Daughter has given up
Snapchat... and the results could
give other parents pause for
thought!!!

Okay, so it was a forced break from Snapchat, because of the constant concerned stance from me and my mother saying 'she is a changed girl because of that phone!'

I had become concerned over time that the drift was widening and I was playing catch up in the emotions department. My daughter was short tempered, with disturbed sleep and was generally difficult to be around. I was witnessing her becoming tranced into a digital world of ideals and perfection. She was agitated and life weighed heavy.

We agreed that I would give her a basic Samsung phone that could not operate the much-obsessed social media apps. Don't get me wrong, it wasn't easy, but neither was spending time with her when she had her phone quite frankly. After the phone hand over, the change was not gradual, it was nearly immediate and dramatic. Within 3 hours she was sitting downstairs for longer, making conversation about school and taking an interest in my working life and swimming. She was also more tolerant with her younger brother, which believe me she doesn't find easy.

The following morning, I had my daughters phone. It was switched on and was bleeping and pinging every 90 seconds or so as it had been doing throughout the previous evening and night. Two hours into the morning, my daughter had a total of 46 notifications that she would have been required to respond to. 8 o'clock that night she had 89 beeps (couldn't say what they were) Streaks ...we will get onto that in a minute! messages, video clips. I was irritated listening to it, never mind opening them and responding.

Streaks!!!! They are a rally that your daughter or son needs to keep going with the friend. A sort of Hi. Hi every day with a photo attached to ALL the contacts on their Snapchat (probably most of her year) but some people do it 6 times a day. If only 10 of the friends do that, it is 60 streaks your son or daughter has to open and maybe respond to even if that person doesn't even raise an eyebrow to her/him in the dinner hall. Young people spend an average of 4 hours on screen time a day, most of this is staring at a phone screen.
DO YOU FEEL TIRED YET? I DO!

My daughters sleep has improved, she reports feeling relieved and more energised. Of course, it is only a temporary break, but I am hoping that when she has experienced the benefits of time away and will be able to use her better judgement when she is again allowed back on the apps.

OK you want to not think about it for a while, its giving you a headache. well we will leave it there, but just so you know, the results are in, she's sat drawing with me at the kitchen table as I write now.

Teenagers, Bullying, Paranoid
Fearful Thinking...Social media
and the fragile sense of self.

My daughter had a 3 month break from social media this year, I wrote a post about it early in my blogging journey, the change in her was dramatic and enjoyable. Two weeks ago, she decided to go back onto Instagram, she is not enjoying it and is toying with the idea of another break.

We have all read as parents the dangers of social media, most of us have experienced our child's distress first hand. We have also heard the argument that social media means the child can't get a break from criticism and being in the spotlight. The photos teenager's post of themselves means they are there for them to agonise over their flaws repeatedly, and for their peers to analyse and comment on.

Comparisons can be made to other people's seemingly perfect lives, perfect bodies, fantastic families, holidays, outfits, academic achievement etc.

When we were in our teens you knew the good things about your friends, but because you truly knew them, you also got a sense of their not so good bits, their struggles, their insecurities and fears. Those friends were in your social circle. Now our teenagers can be 'friends' with up to 700 people on social media. How can they possibly know the not so great bits to balance out a comparison?

My clients say they feel a sense of 'no option than to be on social media', it is no longer about connecting with friends, but checking that those people they consider "friends" are not commenting and talking about them.

When things are said about us in adult life, we have some experience to see us through.

Let's say you get a poor appraisal at work and other people within work talk about that and say things that aren't true or unkind. As an adult, you have other good experiences to bring to mind, you have achieved a family maybe, or you have good friends as a support network, your neighbours think you are a kind and patient person with your children. You can also bring to mind challenges that you have managed well, you have faced daunting situations and come out the other end. The poor appraisal at work is only one part of your life.

In short, we have experiences that define who we are and give us a strong sense of identity. We have a strong anchor.

As teenagers 'friends' and fitting in, is their life. They look to friends to define who they are. In this way, they have a fragile sense of self, a self that can be damaged by repeated cruel comments or an unpredictable exclusion from a peer group.

If your teenager is going through this and they have been open enough to talk about the distress that social media brings to their lives, you could do the following things:

·   Talk to your child over two or three days, find out the facts. Is there some online bullying happening?

Bullying is defined as behaviour that is repeated, intended to hurt both physically and emotionally including teasing, name calling and making threats.

·   If this is the case and is happening within school time, I would say that you need to contact school in the first instance. Quote the definition of bullying and ask to see a copy of the anti-bullying policy. Please do this in writing as all written documentation needs to be presented to Ofsted when an inspection takes place.

This concentrates their attention on the issue and motivates the school to resolve the issue.

· If it is happening outside of school time, I would advise that you contact the parents by email or text. If this seems scary, please ask yourself how you would feel or what you would do if you received an email stating that your teenager was causing undue distress to somebody else. Hopefully you would feel empathetic and determined to sort it out. If you don't feel this way then your reading the wrong blog! (yep controversial)

· Talk to your teenager about bullying, how it effects the young person and their families. Here is a link to a short video about being bullied and how it feels. Maybe all teenagers should be shown it.

http://www.lbc.co.uk/radio/audio-video/children-lbc-bullying-affected-mental-health/

After you have managed the situation and hopefully it has come to a good conclusion, you can think about a family friend or a kind neighbour doing some identity/self-esteem work with your teenager.

This is quite a long process and you may have to add to the list as you, or your teenager notice different things within the coming weeks. If your teenager struggles to get started, you can start with all the things I am not. E.g. not cruel, not dishonest, not explosive etc.

It is important you do not provide answers and strongly suggest things. This work has to come from the teenager for them to internalise it and reflect on it. This exercise involves your teenager thinking and documenting the following:

What do you like about yourself, no matter how fleeting?

Example, nice smile, Good at singing, my organisation skills

What positive qualities do you possess? (include qualities that you do not display 100% of the time)

Example, good listener, polite, patient, loyal, supportive, responsible, respectful (you would be surprised how often this is true of your teenager)

What small or big things have you achieved?

Example, lead role in play, sports day achievement, poem published in school newsletter, gymnastics/swimming certificate etc.

What challenges have you faced in life and dealt with?

Example, ill health, parents separating, suffering with anxiety... anything the teenager found really hard.

What skills have you acquired?

Example, Work skills, domestic skills, computer skills, ride a bike, swim backstroke.

What do other people turn to you for?

Example, working out their iPhone, helping people with spelling,

What are my true likes, what topics, activities do I do that excite me, what am I passionate about?

Swimming, Harry Potter films, crafting

This isn't going to totally ease the distress, but it provides the teenager with a blue print of identity. They can look at this list and remind themselves of their resilience in difficult times.

Another suggestion is if you can, negotiate with your teenager that there be an hour in the evening when they don't go on their phone or social media. It is healthy to get a break and loosen that tight focus of friends, image, school, relationship breakup's.

Social media and bullying is always going to be distressing for the teenager and their family but being proactive in addressing it is the answer. What is also part of the answer being if you have an honest, frank conversation about what bullying does to a young person, promote empathy, model empathy to your teenager and keep the communication lines open.

*Be vigilant soon to be year 9
parents, there may be some bad
choices in the friend department
coming.*

Up until this point you may have had quite a bit of sway in regards to your child's friends. In primary you could make the excuses regarding tea invites and parties; your teenager may have stuck with the same set of friends from primary in year 7 and part of 8 of secondary school. Then year 9 comes and it seems that yourself and your teenager are talking a different language about friends.

This is the time to be on the ball about all things, the peak period for peer influence is 13. This is when they are experiencing themselves as a truly separate other. They are flexing their autonomy muscles and seeing where the limit is. In my experience the period after Christmas of year 9 was when I really had to make it clear what I would accept and what I wouldn't. Parents of teenage clients also say the same thing to me. That year 9 is the tipping point or the 'game changer' as one dad said.

The first thing to notice is that they will start to dress like their peer group and more annoyingly, talk like them. Sometimes in a bid to fit in they become an extreme worst version of themselves.

My daughter went through this with a friend in year 9, they were poles apart in their interests and also how seriously they took school and school work. I got a call from school one day about my daughter using bad language. There was a consequence put in place and we moved on.

When I met the friend, she was polite and courteous. Nothing to be troubled about, but my daughter's attention and focus at home and school continued to nose dive. I caught her smoking, school sympathised and suggested that 'she is easily led'. It was a nice way of saying that the friend was making the negative difference.

I knew that cutting the friendship off would only encourage her to want it more. So, at every opportunity I did the following:

- I tried not to sound to judgemental and considered a reasoned point of view to put across.
- I put into place some non-negotiables re sleeping over (she wasn't allowed as the friend was allowed more freedom than my daughter)
- I spoke to my daughter about risky behaviour such as smoking, drinking and drugs (they don't talk about this in school as much anymore, legal highs are the hot topic.
- THIS IS THE MOST IMPORTANT ONE. At every opportunity given to me by my daughter, I emphasized the differences between them. When she moaned about her, when she celebrated her, when they both chose there GCSE options, when she struggled to get on with the friend's other friends. I pointed out how different they were and that maybe that was the cause of the frustration. I suggested she was more responsible and could see that there were differences and then I left it alone.
- I made sure we were doing stuff in the holidays.
- I encouraged her to get a job.
- I asked school to speak to the teachers and maybe suggest they were in different work groups in class.
- I pointed out that she was exhausted with the high drama that the friend always had going on.

Eventually after a break from snapchat (my daughter's choice) and a really honest discussion about the way other people were starting to see her. She chose to back off from the friend, at this point I encouraged sleep overs with old friends. She helped me more with general stuff and I was flexible in my response to her making arrangements with other friends and wanting lifts.

What I am wanting is for my daughter to feel I am responsive and that I have set clear boundaries in an assertive way while still listening to her views and wishes. I don't want her to feel I emotionally control her, but that I am flexible in my approach.

Is your teenager using cannabis?
These are the tell-tale signs...

Nearly 40% of teenagers in the UK said they have tried substances including cannabis and ecstasy, teenagers in Britain are more likely to have taken illegal substances than youngsters anywhere else in Europe.

Most young people try cannabis in teenage years, parents expect it, it is a part of growing up. However, if 'trying' turns into regular use, that is causing you to worry about your teenager. Maybe it will help to communicate with your teenager

The following signs could be an indication that your teenager is developing a dependence.

·   He/she becomes not motivated, loses an interest... Always been into sport, cars, playing the guitar, mountain biking etc... but now can't be bothered doing the activity, instead watches these things on YouTube. Is not motivated to get to college on time, not motivated to earn some pocket money. Generally, turns into someone you would consider lazy (yes, I know, I mean lazy above and beyond the normal teenage limits of lazy).

·   Starts to talk about weed in terms of it being used for good causes, medical marijuana, healing properties etc., tentatively suggests the law is stupid, pointless

·   A change in friendship group – not always an indicator of drug or drink use, but if he suddenly decides his old friends are boring or they have had a falling out over something unexplained then this is an indicator that they no longer share the same interests.

·   Angry outbursts, really out of proportion reactions to things suggested.

·   Increased appetite.

·   Poor time sense, when it hasn't been an issue previously.

·   Paranoia- with the theme of intrusion. *You're always poking your nose in, stop interrogating me.*

·   This may be surprising to you, but research has shown that if your teenager is academically clever then they are at more risk of habitually smoking drugs, here is a link to the article about the study

http://www.telegraph.co.uk/education/2017/02/23/clever-teenagers-twice-likely-smoke-cannabis-due-curious-minds/

·   A sudden drop in academic performance.

·   The obvious ones but worth a mention are…finding lighters, papers in pockets, posters/stickers with cannabis leaf, immersing themselves in Bob Marley, grime, cannabis smoking culture.

I am not stereotyping the "weed smoker" characteristics, I understand that some of the things listed are unrelated to cannabis smoking.

So, what to do if you believe your teenager is developing a dependence to cannabis?

· First of all, educate yourself, gaining knowledge about a subject can make us feel more on top of things and sometimes lessen our anxiety.

· Make sure before you have the conversation with your teenager, that you are in a calm and responsive mood. Not reactive and oversensitive. If you used cannabis when you were young, think about how much of this you would like to disclose and in what way it will benefit your teenager knowing.

i. Use open ended questions that encourages reflection and expression of feelings.

ii. Acknowledge their point of view.

iii. Be honest and open about your expectation around cannabis use and why you feel that way.

iv. Exaggerating the negatives of cannabis use and lecturing about it will not counteract the experiences the teenager views as positive.

· Take the time to learn why your teenager is using cannabis. For the feeling, to escape, manage anxiety, to fit in or to calm hyperactivity.?

· The most important thing is to keep in mind when communicating with your teenager is that ultimately our aim is to find ways to encourage our teenagers to want to communicate with us. Make sure they have the assurance that they won't get an overblown reactive response.

Ultimately depending on what the young person says regarding usage, i.e.

Frequency

Smoking at school/college

Need a joint to get to sleep etc.,

Then the aim is to reduce usage. For example, try and help your teenager to not smoke it before activities that require cognitive functioning such as classes, homework, exams, driving. If your teenager is smoking cannabis to alleviant anxiety or escape painful memories then professional help is appropriate in the form of counselling

From my experience (I used to work in a therapeutic community for people with substance misuse) If your teenager says they smoke 3 a day, it more likely they are smoking 6. You need to know the starting point to help your teenager with reduced usage.

The teenager has got to be wanting a change on some level. If you would like to find out more about the topic of change, it is worth researching the cycle of change and also a book titled 'Freedom from Addiction. The Secret Behind Successful Addiction Busting' (The Human Givens approach book 2)

ATTUNING TO YOUR TEENAGER

What do teenagers really want to tell their parents, how best can we respond?

Parent: What's wrong with you, your quiet?

Teenager: Nothing, I'm just tired.

Parent: No, it's not that, it's something else, come on what's wrong?

Teenager: God, nothing, I'm fine I just feel a bit anxious that's all.

Parent: Well what you anxious about, come on tell me.

Teenager: Nothing, just stuff

Parent: Well come on tell me, I may be able to help.

Teenager: You can't help. I'm going upstairs, I can't be bothered!!

Recognise this Parents??

It can leave us feeling rejected and unaware of what is happening in our teenager's life. The practical reasons for poor communication such as other siblings being around, long working hours and TV and video gaming can be hard to navigate. When you teenager hits a rough patch, and believes you won't understand, then their distress can quickly escalate.

Of course, keeping secrets from your parents is nothing new, I could have won a prize in it. We have all done it and still do it as parents today. Lots of parents don't tell their own parents about their teenager's misdemeanours, why...because you can't be bothered to listen to the 'lectures'

3 out of 5 parents believe communication with their teenager is getting worse, and half of all teenagers believe they cannot discuss their problems with their parents. Boys have a harder time expressing themselves to their parents than girls. There is a key age in teenage years where communication for both girls and boy's changes and it becomes harder for the parent to attune. This age seems to be 13. Only half of 13-year olds feel they can talk to their parents, compared with 70 percent of 12-year olds. They need you more in year 7 and the start of year 8 in secondary school, after this they grow more confident in their friendships and it seems to them that parents are dinosaurs that have never experienced anything.

When our teenagers believe we won't understand, what they are really experiencing is being interrupted, advice giving, feeling judged and us reacting to situations in an overblown way. This is generally too much verbal intrusion from someone who has failed to read between the lines.

My teenage clients believe (sometimes wrongly) … we as parents are in the bargain basement bin of understanding our own children, why? Because we are over 40, we are bracketed in to the category of teachers at school.

It is hard for us as parents to just listen. We have helped pack the school bag, helped our children form friendships, we have done a whole host of practical things to help our children along the way. Attentive and non-judgemental listening is really hard because the worry is all consuming. Trying to find the meaning in something, requires us to zoom out and reflect those feelings back to our teenager's. It's a bit like finding a theme amongst a hold host of words.

Can I just say that listening is my job and although I have good communication with my teenage daughter, sometimes the worry takes over and it all goes wrong. It's a hard thing to do.

So, if I'm to use my research from my teenage clients: the thing that your teenager really wants to tell you is one of two things, that sometimes (although you try hard) your listening isn't great and they feel frustrated trying to make themselves understood.

The second thing it may be is they can't share what they want to share because they have a sense of burdening you, they have the impression you won't cope.

The counselling relationship is powerful because the client has a sense of bringing heavy stuff that will be emotionally held. Off course there are other powerful components such as it's somebody separate from the family, empathic qualities etc, but being understood is a powerful thing.

So, some top tips for listening:

Sometimes you do need to give them clear advice and guidance, but only when you have truly listened and reflected back. Don't set off for your destination before you've read the map!

· No opinions, thoughts or conclusions until the teenager has really said all they need to say.

· Check your understanding by asking 'do you mean', 'are you saying', 'it sounds like you feel'.

· Ask open questions if you need to ask any at all.

· Be as available as possible

·   Ask yourself what would I feel if I was in that position/had experienced that?

There is a kindle download book that may be useful to you titled *the art of active listening: How to double your communication skills in 30 days*. If you don't have a kindle you can borrow any book from the library on communication skills that will give you an idea on active listening.

The task of active listening becomes even harder when the topic of conversation is you or dad or step dad or a sibling because we as parents feel we have to defend ourselves to save us from tolerating the uncomfortable feelings that these conversations bring. Obviously when we are in the firing line just because your teenager feels like it, that is not ok. However, when the teenager repeatedly brings the same theme/message/feeling or reaction to something we may need to stop and listen, think about it overnight and respond the following evening after school (not following morning...bad idea)

I read the following text by Winnicott this weekend which I thought I would share with you here:

"theirs is the task of tolerating the interaction of several disparate phenomena- their own immaturity, their own puberty and changes, their own idea of what life is about and their own ideals and

aspirations; add to this their personal disillusionment about the world of grown-ups – which for them seems to be essentially a world of compromise, of false values, and infinite distraction from the main theme...From being comes doing, there can be no do before be, and this is their message to us".

All the above to think about...and that is before Instagram and snapchat!

If you have enjoyed this blog please like and share and also share on Facebook.

Winnicott.D 1986, *Home is where we start from*, penguin, London

How to emotionally meet your teenager...explore your own reactions

Before I go on with this post, I would like to say that the following is what I aim for, it doesn't always go to plan, no one is a perfect parent all of the time!

It is too easy for us as parents to hold onto the feelings generated when we argue with our teenagers. Teenagers say some horrible things when they are angry, and they are usually angry when they can't get what they want. We dwell on what is said, we find it hard to comprehend the unreasonableness of our teenager.

We think and say loudly sometimes...*what is going on, what planet is he/she on?*

They are on the planet of "self-serving, self-centred, peer orientated, urgent gratification, my needs matter more than anyone's planet".

It is really really hard not to be hurt by their actions or some of the things they say in a temper.

When my daughter was younger (primary school age) tantrums did not happen often, but when they did occur, they were pretty turbulent. Sometimes within these she would say *'your mean, I don't like you'* and my response was always *'well that's a shame because I really love you'* this used to dampen down the energy somewhat, now instead of using those words (although I do tell her I love her every morning) My actions, more than my words, say I love her.

I try and keep my conscious attention on what's happening, instead of being all churned up with emotion.

So, after an argument or an outburst I do still do the following things:

· Go and collect her when she has missed the bus/spent the bus fare. Car journeys seem to be a place where things get ironed out (it's to do with little eye contact)

· After a big explosion...I leave it 20 minutes and go up to her room, make it clear the explosion is not ok, but is there anything I can do to help?

· When she has done something really silly or dangerous (summer term this year), I put in the consequences and then get on with relating to her in exactly the same way as before. I don't hold grudges. I am the grown up and have been on the planet much longer than she has. I try and respond, not react. By doing this I am more aware of my daughters needs and feelings, I can zoom out from situations and not feel bad afterwards about impulsive arguments.

Everyone makes mistakes...teenagers even more so (it's a brain development thing).

· I still ask her to come food shopping with me, I like the company and she has some valuable ideas on meals.

· Try to understand, try not to make judgments, don't make some throwaway comment starting 'oh right what you going to do now, blah blah blah.

· Perhaps most importantly, don't make judgements about friends and boyfriends in conversation after arguments. Your teenager is not interested in your views on friendships, they think you are out of date.

What all these things do is offer the olive branch and teach your child that they are loved regardless of behaviour, A behaviour plan is the thing that irons out behaviour. Love and understanding is what keeps them close.

Are you divorcing or separating
from your partner, this is what my
teenage client's say has helped?

I won't write about how hard it is to separate, you know that if you're experiencing it. Here are the 10 things that has helped the separation go smoothly for the kids. For whatever reason, I know the following things are not always possible, I just thought I would share what my teenage clients think.

These 10 things made the separation easier for the kids.

1) Their feelings were heard and respected and they felt comfortable to ask about arrangements that directly affected them.

2) The young person appreciated that mum and dad briefly told them if they were having a bad day because of it, so they didn't wonder if some of the mood was due to them.

3) They didn't want to know every detail of the reasons for the separation particularly if there had been an affair.

4) Gradual introduction of major changes, so they were able to focus on different aspects of their own life. New house, new partner, new siblings was greatly spaced out.

5) Flexibility was very important to all my clients, being able to say to mum or dad that they wouldn't be visiting that weekend as they had a social event planned with friends was a relief.

6) Both mum and dad have a support network such as their parents, friends, siblings. This allowed my clients to feel their parents were supported and they didn't have to comfort parents and worry about their wellbeing. Also, the teenager had someone who was an adult that they could talk to about the separation.

7) My clients who had step parents appreciated that they were supportive towards them, but not intrusive and 'try and be my mum, I've got a mum'

8) They were glad the arrangement was to stay with the other parent on certain nights and not a week with mum and then a week with dad. Most of my clients felt that it was too long a time to not see the other parent and organisation issues would not allow it to work.

9) Teenagers appreciated that both parents presented as coping because it would 'feel weird to comfort my dad'

10) Teenagers are glad when parents can communicate in a civil way, they don't want to be used as the messenger.

SCHOOL ADVICE

*Is your child starting secondary
school this time ...Here is the
important stuff to keep in mind?*

Most important for parents, above all else (ironed on name tags, P.E kit etc) is to check in with themselves, are you anxious? Are you transmitting that anxiety through asking too many questions, keep fussing and checking your child is ok?

This stuff that parents do is perfectly understandable, but what this does is send the message to the young person that there is 'something' to worry about. The child begins to feel/think that *'maybe this school stuff is* scary *and maybe I won't cope'.*

For some parents, their own school experience was not a great one. Maybe they felt anxious, they were excluded or bullied, however that will not necessarily be the same for your child and it might be useful to think about what makes you and your child different (characteristics, resilience, family set up, life circumstances etc.)

Practical tips

Don't plan much in the month of September, everything should be low key, homework routine, sleep routine and provide enough down time to process the change.

Listen to worries, don't try to solve them. The child does not want you to come up with a solution, they want you to understand their worries, attune to them and imagine what it feels like to have those worries. It may be useful for parents to think of a time when you were experiencing a huge change that took you out of your comfort zone and induced feelings of anxiety and inadequacy whilst trying to process the loss of something familiar (your child will be thinking about primary and processing that as a loss in some way)

These worries are best listened to in the car sometimes when eye to eye contact is not required.

Travel – Some parents feel more comfortable taking the child to school on the first day, that's great as you can have a chat in the car and keep it as relaxed as possible. For the return journey, my advice would be that your child travels home on the bus if that is the long-term travel arrangement. The next day, he goes on the bus to and from school. The school bus IS the start of the school day, its where friendships are formed, homework is copied and they get to find their place in the school pecking order.

This is an obvious one. If you have a friend with an older child in the school can an arrangement be made that he will try and find your child at dinnertime (in a casual way) and check he is ok. You could offer a money incentive to the older child, not much (£1) but it may be a motivator for him/her to stick her head round the dinner hall door.

If your child starts to suffer with stomach ache, headaches, dizziness, light headed then they are probably starting with consistent anxiety. Again, a car journey conversation may open up a discussion about the anxieties. If it is friend related (lack of friends) YOU NEED TO CONTACT SCHOOL and speak to pastoral. There will be groups and clubs in break time and dinner time that your child can try. The pastoral people will know of other children struggling and they can suggest that they buddy up, they may never be lifelong friends but it can carry your child through the transition period.

Some other big changes that your child will need to navigate:

- Make 3 copies of the timetable. They will lose them in the early days

- Make sure you child gets a phone number of somebody in his subjects for when they are unsure of homework that has been set.

- Encourage your child to get into the habit of writing info/homework in his planner before he stands up to leave the class, as soon as he is out the door the chances of it going in the planner are slim.

·   Packing different books on different days (keep the timetable pinned on the wall near the front door)

·   Different teachers with different teaching styles and varying degrees of patience. Speak to your child about the possibility that there will be more shouting from teachers, but make it clear it is not directed at them it is a way to gain attention from chatty pupils. NOT ALL TEACHERS WILL USE THE BEHAVIOUR POINT SYSTEM IN THE SAME WAY!

·   Dinner money and dinner line, food is no longer bought to them by a smiling dinner lady, they need to be organised and get in the queue at the earliest opportunity.

Life will seem hard for them in the first few weeks, lots to remember, lots to organize so try to keep the questions to a minimum (in my experience they haven't got the brain space and can't be bothered to converse at length)

The most important thing is to transmit the message that this is just the next phase, you understand it is hard and different, but so are lots of things we try to master at first. Be as relaxed as you can with it and the anxiety will dissipate for both you and your child.

Starting secondary...Strategies to ensure homework is completed

A clear routine around homework is the most important thing when starting secondary and year 7 is the time to start it.

There will not be any homework in the first week for the new starter, they may be asked to read something or write a small paragraph but in the main it will start to come midway into the second week. Here are some pointers to start as you mean to go on.

Location

Find the right location for completing homework, from my experience their bedroom is the wrong choice as there are too many distractions, and many children do not have a desk in their room to lay out their books. The dining room is a good choice, away from other children and the noise of the house, alternatively the kitchen table is an option after everybody has eaten.

Timing

Your child/teenager ideally needs to get into the habit of doing homework at the same time each day. Some children need a break straight after school (and they may join after school clubs anyway), but if they can carry on the momentum of the school day and complete it as soon as they get in, that is great. If your child does need the break, straight after the evening meal is also a good time. The child has had enough of a break, but it's not too late that they have become mentally tired.

Planning

It is a little unrealistic that you will sit down and look at all the subjects and plan the homework for the week but help your child out by looking at the description of the tasks and estimate how long it will take. Time perception is not a strong point at this age, the young person can't help that, it's about brain development.

Incentives

Not everyone agrees there should be incentives, some people believe that children should do their homework because they are required to...end of. I get that, but if we as parents think like that, we are also saying that a child or teenager can see the 'long game', IF I DO THIS NOW IT WILL BENEFIT ME IN THIS WAY LATER. Well they don't think like this most of the time, which is why they do risky behaviour. Another brain development thing (if you would like to know more, then please check out my workshops on teenage behaviour)

https://www.facebook.com/pg/TalkingToTeenagers/events/?ref= page_internal

So what incentives work best. Pretty short-term ones, something like a point system that adds up to money for the weekend or game vouchers.

BUYING A GAME FOR YOUR CHILD BECAUSE HE WANTS ONE AND HIS FRIEND HAS IT, BUT HE HASN'T DONE HIS HOMEWORK IS SENDING OUT THE WRONG MESSAGE.

Daily incentives such as:

a hot chocolate with marshmallows and squirty cream after 3 homework subjects complete.

15 minutes extra on the Xbox etc.

Is this bribery? Absolutely it is, it goes on in adult exchanges as well, that's what performance bonuses are about. You will benefit from it because you are not called into school to talk about your daughter's lack of effort and your daughter will benefit because she has done her homework and is learning new things.

 If you are a house that doesn't have loads of routine built in, the best option is for your child/teenager to attend homework club twice a week at school and do an hour slot at home on a Saturday morning. This way school have some input as well, school recognise that your child is trying academically, and if there are other issues then your child is known to teachers for good reasons.

Lastly encourage your child to write down the task in the planner before they stand up and leave the class...If it is not in the planner, you probably will not get to know there is homework, or if you do the child may be not be able to recall the important detail.

Do you have a child doing their GCSE's next year?

This is how the hard sell from school is affecting their future and what you can do to help.

Nearly every child in the UK in years 10 and 11 will go back to school in September having at least one assembly a week on G.C.S.E and attainment, and a form period where teachers start of on one topic, but by the end of the 15 minutes in form... somehow, we have ended up talking about ambition and commitment.

Some clients reported feeling sick before the assemblies or form time!

How do I know this?

I worked in a secondary school for 2 years, in that school's counselling provision team, I am now an adolescent therapist in private practice seeing young people who, most of the time, are anxious and wired about the G.C.S.E process.

"THIS IS YOUR LAST CHANCE TO GET IT RIGHT"

"IF YOU DON'T GET THE RESULTS, LET ME TELL YOU, YOU ARE ON THE BOTTOM OF THE PILE"

"EVERY EMPLOYER WILL FOCUS ON G.C.S.E S, FACT"

This is what most young people are hearing in school!

How is it helpful it to whip up such a frenzy that the young person either works themselves into the ground, or switches off completely? The children's charity NSPCC has recently reported a surge in the number of teenagers seeking help through their support services, specifically due to exam stress and anxiety. Don't get me wrong the teachers are not to blame, the league tables are.

Once pupils return to school after the Christmas break in year 11 they pretty much have revision classes for every lesson, by the time the Easter break comes there has been 390 hours of revision completed, but for some schools this isn't enough. Two different clients at different schools that I have worked with were actively encouraged to attend a revision week over the Easter break in school this year.

The predicted grade is a bug bear with my clients, they say it has no resemblance to their current capability and it sets up an expectation to parents which adds more pressure.

I'd just like to make the point that Finland send their children to school for the least number of hours a week than any other country in Europe, they also do not introduce any formal assessment or exam until they are age 17, and yet it is one of the top achieving countries of academia in Europe.

Believe me, the pressure starts at around March time in year 10 and builds like steam in a pressure cooker until exam season of year 11.

As a parent, can you remember the good old days of exams, when you sat out in the sun on exam leave and met up with your mates under the guise of group revision. This is unthinkable for the young person studying today. It is drilled into students that if they do have exam leave (not all schools do) most weekdays need to be filled with a solid five-hour session of revision.

The following are a list of things you can do to balance out the now internalised expectation of sleep, revise, eat, repeat.

· Exam timetable – When the exam timetable is sent home, examine it and draw another one up with your teenager, less a quarter of the total revision time.

·   Distraction- If your teenager is forward thinking enough to admit that distraction onto social media is one of their problems in staying focused. You can use social media blockers such as https://freedom.to/ or http://antisocial.80pct.com/ while revising, so social media checking is not an option.

·   Varied activities – when anybody focuses on one thing constantly, perspective is lost. From January time onwards make a promise with your teenager that you will go to the cinema every couple of weeks and go for a walk (a proper mapped walk) the other week. There is an old Zen saying *"You should sit in nature for 20 minutes a day, unless you're busy and then you should sit for an hour"* You are looking to enjoy things that involve most of the senses. Swimming is also a good stress buster.

·   Fiction input – When teenagers enter years 10 and 11, they have tended to stop reading fiction, so they are either reading subject text books or they are on social media. At Christmas time do some research on a good book trilogy on amazon, buy it and give as a Christmas present and suggest half an hour before bed that their phone goes on airplane mode and they complete 20 minutes of reading.

·   Interruption- After a lengthy revision period, actively interrupt it and ask the young person to do something else...This is particularly relevant to perfectionist who can't gauge when enough really is enough.

· Choose what info to take in – nearer the time, friends will be saying how much they have revised, what mark they got in the mock. How well they did in a past paper, how they have done all the past papers for every subject EVER in the history of the universe. This is not helpful, and the sooner your child decides not to take it on board, tune out and get on with their own thing the better his/her anxiety levels will be.

Nearer the time of exams when there is high anxiety and they are cramming in revision, reassure you teenager that they can't know what they don't know. That they have done the most possible to raise the chances of success. Do a checklist

- Have they done past papers (still the best indicator of what will be on the exam)

- Have they stuck to YOUR revised revision timetable?

- Have they taken enough breaks so they have remained objective and feel relaxed but in control?

Then they can say they are prepared.

A last note to parents... It is important to remember that although we want the very best for our teenagers and we really want them to feel proud of their achievements, we also don't want to get sucked into the school's narrative. It is an important time yes, but what is equally important to remember is that it is just one aspect of the child. British education is not a holistic endeavour unfortunately. What matters even more than exams are our teenager's mental health.

Ambition

Yes, you can be anything you want to be, with hard work, exceptional luck, patience, persistence and natural skill...X-Factor auditions are full, how about the BAE systems apprenticeship?

I went to a Christmas singing concert last week to watch my daughter and others sing 70's and 80's disco tracks as that was the theme of the concert. The concert was organised by the local singing school. They all did well, some as young as five braving the glaring stage lights to perform a song, I couldn't do it.

My daughter has natural singing talent, after the show she asked me for my feedback, I said she had done really well, although she could have given it a bit more oomph. She didn't speak to me for the rest of the night.

The uncomfortable reality is... she practised the song at singing school for a few Saturday mornings, learning the lyrics and timing of the song but then she relied on the assumption that she would wing it, only practising for half an hour for the 3 days before the concert. I know you will think I sound like a pushy mum, but it isn't that. It's this dislike of instant reward for little work, a message that X-Factor and You Tube transmit.

"one day you will be discovered if you just sit there and radiate talent"

My daughter actually wants to be a police woman, she wants to go to university and gain a degree and enter the force as a detective. Singing may be a side line, to fund the ever-increasing University fees.

Nowadays, as a young person, you can really hedge your bets on being famous, as we churn out so much crap where talent and hard work have little to do with celebrity status, that it's a dream you can nearly touch.

In 2010 a poll was conducted where some 1000 UK teenagers aged 16 were asked the question "what you would like to do for your career?" 54% said to be a celebrity. Those teenagers are now 23 years old. I wonder what percentage are on our TV's? Did these teens keep another dream alive alongside "celebrity"?

What happens to our teenagers while they hold on to the dream of being singers, You Tubers, actors? They close the door on the things they may have a natural gift for. What we going to do when there are no scientists to further research on Alzheimer's disease or a welfare assistant to take care of kids on the school lunch, because they are all standing in line waiting to be discovered. Being in the public eye, in entertainment, relies on one thing that we have no practical control over...LUCK

The Nolan sisters were discovered in the Blackpool Cliffs Hotel in 1973, their chart breakthroughs were in 1978 with their biggest hits in 1979...I'm not an expert but I'm guessing that took hard work, exceptional luck, patience, persistence and natural skill. Google The Cliffs Hotel in Blackpool, believe me, The Nolans had a bucket full of luck as well as talent.

If I tell my daughter, she can be anything she wants to be and that doesn't happen, she will search internally to find the reason why, she will feel disappointed, but you need all the components for it to happen. She needs to know that she can increase the chances of it happening by practising the above, but don't expect it. Always have two plan A's working concurrently.

When our kids want to be scientists, but are not brilliant at maths, it is our responsibility to say "let's try something science related that doesn't rely on maths". Don't hammer the maths and hold onto that particular dream.

When our kids want to be singers but don't seem to get better year on year, let's not buy extra lessons and hope that the talent will come, lets focus on learning make-up, hair and stage production aspects.

I will say, just because it's worth saying. That the new chief executive of BAE systems has just negotiated a 7.5 million pay packet and he can go to the supermarket without wearing a hat and wig and the press camping outside his house. Probably more effort, but he had a detailed plan along the way.

10 LESSONS ON ANXIETY THAT WILL BE USEFUL FOR YOU AND YOUR TEENAGER.

Anxiety – The drain on teenager's happiness and well- being, here are some practical tips!

I recently read that anxiety is experienced when there is a fear of a particular outcome and you feel you will be unable to cope with that outcome. This is true in part I suppose for adults experiencing intermittent anxiety, but for teenagers I have worked with, the feeling is different. For teenager's suffering with anxiety it is a baseline feeling, it infuses every waking hour (sleeping is an escape).

It is the feeling that your lungs are never really full when you take that deep breath.

It is the feeling of never being fully relaxed when out and about and you just want the time to pass to be home and to lie on your bedroom floor.

It is the dread of somebody starting to tell you a funny story that you can't concentrate on because your heart is beating out of your chest and it's enough to think about coping and nothing is funny anyway.

It is the thing that makes everything hard work, miserable, it makes you avoid things you used to enjoy and you resent it for that and it makes you angry, but that makes you anxious again.

There are some practical things that you can do to dampen down that anxious state. I'm not going to talk about grounding and breathing techniques (both probably need an adult to introduce and guide you through these coping strategies)

Instead I am going to talk about activities that make your front brain (prefrontal cortex) come 'online' and take the strength away from the amygdala (emotional brain) which is the part of the brain that is activating the fight or flight response and is pumping huge amounts of adrenalin into your body that is going unused. We will talk about this unused adrenalin later on.

Sleep is one of the most important resources when managing anxiety, lack of sleep can severely impact the way we feel and our ability to manage 'well enough' when we start to feel anxious. Ideally you are looking to get to sleep by 11.30 and sleep till 7.30... I know what you're going to say, '*I can't get to sleep because of anxiety*' and we will also get to that in a minute.

So, things that get the pre-frontal cortex on line have to be neutral enough in emotion (don't get the amygdala going) but interesting enough to engage you cognitively, keep you interested without rousing emotion. Such as

§ You tube: bird watching, birds nesting, springwatch, Osprey videos, Blue Planet programme

§ A popular one that works well is an episode of The Simpsons, totally unrelated to real life, funny and off the wall. Doesn't take itself too seriously and gives a break from serious stuff for a while. Trust me it works!

§ Radio 4 extra, you can choose a topic that slightly interests you, yes, I know radio 4 is boring and for old folk but it's good for the early hours when you can't get back to sleep for a while.

§ You tube: Search 'the most satisfying video ever' mix ups of things being created or destructed in a clever slow-motion way.

§ Wind in the willows on audiobook

Lastly, when we are anxious are bodies are readied for action by the fight or flight response which pumps our bodies with adrenalin that we don't discharge. Exercise is a way to rid the body of that adrenalin, settling down the response systems, allowing us to feel less jittery and calmer. Please remember that is needs to be the kind of exercise that gets you out of breath and a bit sweaty.

And a note for girls, keep the dates of your menstrual cycle on a calendar or diary, anxiety peaks around 5 days before your period and if you do this you will know the reason for the panicky anxious feeling.

*s*ocial anxiety: Don't talk to me....
I'm not shy, I'm petrified!

A teenage male client recently explained to me that social anxiety for him is the feeling that a big bright stage light is on you, following you about the minute you step out of the house and into the public arena.

He then said in a quiet voice '*quite honestly, I'd rather not live at all than live like this for the rest of my life. Who lives like this, I'm pathetic*'

The answer is that more young people live with this 'disorder' (don't like that term) than any other anxiety related illness. Lifetime prevalence rates of up to 12% have been reported, compared with lifetime prevalence estimates for other anxiety disorders of 6% for generalised anxiety disorder, 5% for panic disorder, 7% for post-traumatic stress disorder (PTSD) and 2% for obsessive-compulsive disorder (OCD).

The distress felt by this, is not feeling just a little shy, just a little introverted. My clients feel the constant fear of being negatively judged and rejected and humiliated in some way. People suffering with social anxiety feel inferior, inadequate, not likeable and in teenagers they feel they are weird.

Activities such as using a telephone in public, working while being observed, ordering a coffee can literally induce terror in some people. The impact on my teenage client's interpersonal relationships whether romantic or friendships is far reaching and isolating.

A specific social anxiety would be the fear of speaking in front of groups (only), whereas people with generalized social anxiety are anxious and scared in all social situations.

If you or your teenager is plagued by worry, indecision, self-blame and anticipatory anxiety (worrying beforehand what will happen in a particular encounter) in most life situations then this means a generalized form of anxiety is at play. This is the most common form in teenagers.

Avoidance and safety behaviours

By the time teenagers seek help they have pretty much started to avoid most interactions and as a result their world has narrowed in focus and they find themselves lonely and emotionally alone. When my clients first start counselling they have been using safety behaviours to get them through interactions for quite a long time (how else could school be bearable)? These behaviours just about get them through, but actually as much as the teenager thinks these are helpful, they actually prevent new learning from taking place.

It goes something like this. *'I got through that because I stayed on the edge of the group, I didn't speak about myself, I talked less and didn't give eye contact etc.'*

These things that you do to try and avoid embarrassment in front of others. Although it may seem like doing these things helps to reduce your anxiety, in the long run what you are doing is actually maintaining your fear.

Simply put...it is a pernicious cycle that reinforces itself!!

I work very frequently with clients experiencing social anxiety and quite often they have experienced an unpredictable isolating/rejecting episode in school, which had a dramatic and distressing impact on them that they dealt with mostly alone. This is NOT ALWAYS the case but is a theme I have recognized the more I work with teenage social anxiety.

Social anxiety can be worked with in a phased structured way with a fully trained therapist and the results can be liberating, alternatively there is a good book on amazon that you could work through with the help of an adult (Aunty or family friend would be my suggestion NOT PARENTS) https://www.amazon.co.uk/Shyness-Social-Anxiety-Workbook-Teens-ebook/dp/B0082BXIAI/ref=sr_1_2?ie=UTF8&qid=1502540161&sr=8-2&keywords=teenagers+social+anxiety#

While you work through your social anxiety it is important to motivate yourself to stay in the 'goldilocks zone' anxiety provoking enough for new learning but not so terrifying that you are forced into blind panic. The sooner social anxiety is recognized and worked on, the less hardwired those behaviours become. The impact on teenagers cannot be overstated. Like with any support to work through mental health issues, the results can be life changing.

'Everybody form your own groups.'...SCHOOL SOCIAL ANXIETY HELL!

Social anxiety typically begins early to mid-adolescence, the median age onset is in fact 13 years of age. School can be unbearable for teenagers experiencing social anxiety, a time when physical changes are happening, people are forming friendship groups and the drift from parents is naturally widening.

Teenagers can find themselves lonely and emotionally alone.

So, teenagers take note, the following things are contributing factors in anxiety you may feel in social situations.

<u>Self-focused behaviour</u>

When all your attention is focused inwards, you are concentrating on things such as '*how anxious do I appear*' '*can they see I am shaking*' '*am I appearing normal*'. These thoughts block the natural flow of conversation, as does thinking what you are going to say when the other person has said what they want to say. This can be taken as you not being interested.

Social performance expectations

This is about the young person thinking a conversation has to be a certain way.

I need to be confident, I need to be interesting, I need to be witty I am sure this have been reinforced by the term 'banter' and that every young person believes they should be the next Russell Howard, turning out funny quips and being the life and soul of the gathering. It is ok to have nothing to contribute to the conversation and sit quietly, this aids reflective thinking and shows you are truly listening.

People with social anxiety sometimes feel that pauses in conversation are a sign it isn't going well. Pauses ARE a natural part of conversation, without them people feel they are being talked at.

Core beliefs

These are quite hard wired and they take some work to change, examples of negative social core beliefs are '*I'm boring*' '*people don't tend to like me*' '*I don't fit in*' These are beliefs that have been formed over years through bad experiences in social situations, but don't reflect what your positive qualities are as a person. However, these thoughts totally influence your social interactions.

How you think about others

How you evaluate other people's intentions has a direct influence on the fear you feel in social situations, such as '*people are critical*' '*people are always judging others*' '*people are cruel*' This is often the case in teenagers nowadays where everyone is grouped into the popular, sporty, nerdy groups. The popular kids have the same worries, trust me, they have just chosen a different defence tactic (loud and shouty)!

How you think about disapproval from others

Ultimately this is about rejection, *if others disapprove of me... I will be left out, If I don't agree with other's... I will be excluded, to embarrass myself in front of others would be dreadful*. The impossibility of the situation is that those things are happening now, people with social anxiety have isolated themselves. Work can be done to strengthen the young person's resilience around disapproval, but the main work is about them learning that disapproval is not the end of the world.

These thinking habits can be worked on with a fully trained therapist or alternatively, young people can work through their social anxiety with the use of the book below, and an aunty or close family friend (I wouldn't recommend a parent)

The Shyness and Social Anxiety Workbook for Teens: CBT and ACT Skills to Help You Build Social Confidence by Jennifer Shannon (Author), Doug Shannon (Illustrator), Christine Padesky (Foreword)

Anxiety learning – potential causes

I would like to start this series of blogs on anxiety by saying that I have suffered anxiety too large degrees, mostly in my 20's and recently at 41, when I had become overwhelmed by taking too much on. This episode was short lived because after my training I had learnt to recognise the signs of anxiety and took steps to alleviate it and manage my self-care better.

My 20's anxiety was a different story, there was an accumulation of stress through wrong choices, parent bereavement in my teens (Age 14) and an overriding feeling of lowered coping capacity (basically a belief that I couldn't cope with what life threw at me.)

This summary is a simplified expression of a difficult time, I don't want you to misunderstand me. There are many causes of anxiety in adolescence and adulthood. Some causes are from early trauma, from a traumatic event in adulthood and some are genetic. Today we are going to learn about all different causes of anxiety, to allow you to consider what different factors may have contributed to your anxiety or that of your teenager.

Genetic

From what is known at this time, it is suggested that some people inherit a personality type that influences you to be overly anxious.

This is a reactive, capricious, unsettled personality that is easily triggered by vaguely hostile stimulus. Compelling evidence of this comes from studies of anxiety in identical twins. If one identical twin has an anxiety condition, the probability of the other identical twin developing anxiety ranges from 31 to 88 per cent depending on what study you choose to read.

Research into behaviour and the role genetics play has begun to investigate the seventeen chromosomes, that is a gene in charge of serotonin. This gene is shorter in length in people that suffer with anxiety, people with the long form of the gene have to some extent a resilience to anxiety despite childhood and adult stress. (Bourne, 2005)

 Other factors are:

Parents are overly protective and do some anxious parenting

This is where parents (because they are anxious themselves) look for and point out most of the negative possibilities in any scenario. Such as:

'oh, don't forget your school bag, if you forget that you may get a detention'

'be careful on that swing, if you fall you'll bash your face' 'be very careful when…'

'are you SURE you've remembered everything'

'make sure you ring me because you could break down and freeze to death in this weather'

They also ruminate out loud the negative and traumatic things in current news or relay stories that are sad and negative in nature with no lesson to teach.

The more they transmit this over careful approach, the more the child thinks that the world is a place in which to worry. The child grows up with the notion that the world is a scary place and anxiety is a positive thing, as it "helps" in detecting these potentially dangerous situations.

Suppression of feelings, no fostering of autonomy

This is where parents encourage dependency but also squash your instinctive expression of feelings and assertiveness. Having your own opinion and expressing it was not tolerable to your parent, you were punished or ignored when expressing emotions. Over time children/adolescents who learned to bottle up their feelings and self-expression, become prone to being anxious when wanting to express themselves as adults.

Over critical parents, high standards

The main result of being raised by perfectionist parents, is that the child is always questioning if they are good enough, because of this children are continually trying to please parents to maintain the attachment and receive love (this is the drive we are born with). They need to achieve, look kind, be nice and sacrifice their true feelings. The grown-up child as an adult internalises this becomes critical of themselves and of others. People who experience this usually have rigid rules for living, e.g. *'I should of, I could have, I ought to have'*

Emotional insecurity, developmental trauma

This is a truly difficult and distressing childhood, such as neglect, Physical, sexual and emotional abuse such as in chaotic households where parents are substance users or the parent has their own unresolved trauma meaning they are scary and also incredibly scared themselves.

When raised in a family in these circumstances the child can grow up to avoid feelings and has difficulty building relationships and trusting others. They have an excessive need to please at the expense of their own wellbeing and also have an overwhelming need to control. The impact of these experiences cannot be overstated. People who have experienced these types of abuse are emotionally triggered by explicit (conscious thought/image memories) and implicit memories (automatic body memories and sensations) that trigger the fight or flight response with no knowing consciously what caused it.

They can have patterns of relationships where the push and pull are misunderstood by the other person, but essentially a relationship provides a source of comfort from the other person, but a source of danger as attachment has proved dangerous in the past.

Bullying

Sometimes bullying and anxiety has been downplayed. Bullying has a significant impact on emotional well-being. To be isolated, rejected, excluded with no warning signs and then to be ridiculed and talked about sets the fight or flight system off. It is unpredictable in nature and eventually exhausts the victim who presents as depressed, lonely and hypervigilant. Many young people I see have found the experience of bullying extremely traumatic with a huge effect on their day to day functioning. They don't trust their choices or judgement anymore, they start to believe there is something inherently wrong with them. The world becomes a place that can inflict upset and distress through no actions of their own.

Stress/Life events/turning points

This is stress upon stress due to significant life events that have developed as turning points. Cumulative stress can be caused by unresolved traumas lasting over years. Or It could be marriage problems, work related stress etc.

Life events are experiences that in some cases force us to shuffle our priorities into some different placings. When you look at the extensive list attached most of these events involve loss on some level and interestingly sometimes more responsibility on the individual. Women are twice as likely to suffer from anxiety as men, this may be because the women are the expected care giver, homemaker, part-time employee, finance caretaker. Women sometimes simply feel overwhelmed due to the varied busy roles they are expected to juggle and be good at.

https://www.dartmouth.edu/~eap/library/lifechangestresstest.pdf

A threatening life changing event

Post-traumatic stress disorder may develop after the individual is exposed to a traumatic event that involves actual or threatened death or serious injury. The event may be witnessed more than experienced. Sufferers may experience flashbacks, panic attacks and hypervigilance.

Biological reasons

B12 deficiency/pernicious anaemia – I was diagnosed at 21 and received treatment, my anxiety symptoms lessened somewhat. The lack of this vitamin is known to contribute towards anxiety and depression.

Hypoglycaemia – problems with blood sugar levels

Hyperthyroidism – Excessive release of thyroid hormone

Mitral valve prolapses – A harmless condition that causes heart palpitations

Premenstrual syndrome – Anxiety is worse round this time of the month. It would be worthwhile keeping a diary and if so exercise and taking B vitamins may help.

So, if you would like to look at the reasons for anxiety a bit more. Take the time to look at the life events survey and also consider your anxiety in relation to the family background

Where either parent or family member prone to anxiety?

Did parents encourage exploration or was the world a dangerous place?

Were your parents demanding of you and over critical in their analysis of everything?

Did you feel hurt or rejected, ashamed or feel guilty, but didn't know why?

Where you free to express your opinions and emotions?

Did you experience developmental trauma through abuse, chaotic and inconsistent parenting?

Next time we will look at what keeps anxiety going and what actually happens in the body and brain when anxiety is experienced.

Anxiety learning lesson 2

When we experience anxiety something physical actually happens in the brain as well as the body. It may be helpful for us to look at what happens in the brain when we experience anxiety or panic. The brain is a complex network of different working parts, and certain parts are responsible for certain functions.

When we lived as cavemen thousands and thousands of years ago, we needed the fight or flight response much more than we do today (although it depends what job or past time pursue as to how much you may need to rely on it) This response is what alerts us to threat or danger. It serves to keep us safe and instinctively choose the right course of action in an unsafe situation. The hunter gatherer, in the stone age, needed this response to survive. Now, in this age, we don't need to use it so much. There is no real life-threatening danger in the supermarket or the school playground, like there was running from a charging mammoth a thousand years ago, although I understand it feels like this sometimes

<u>Here is a diagram of the brain.</u>

Where it says the amygdala, we will call the security guard, this part of the brain is extremely old, 50,000 years old and is the emotion part of the brain, it takes care of fear conditioning and is part of the limbic system.

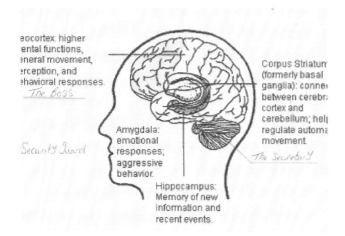

eocortex: higher
ental functions,
:neral movement,
:rception, and
:havioral responses.
The Boss

Security Guard

Amygdala:
emotional
responses;
aggressive
behavior.

Corpus Striatum
(formerly basal
ganglia): conne:
between cerebr:
cortex and
cerebellum; hel;
regulate autom:
movement.
The Secretary

Hippocampus:
Memory of new
information and
recent events.

·   On the diagram, it shows the hippocampus, we will call it the secretary. This part is in charge of long and short-term memory and is also part of the limbic system.

·   The diagram shows the prefrontal cortex, we will call this THE BOSS, this region of the brain is in charge of logic, problem solving, planning, directing attention, inhibiting counterproductive impulses.

·   On the diagram you can see the amygdala, we'll call it the security guard. When a threat is perceived he jumps into action and starts to make us alert to our surroundings, he sends out a message to the rest of the brain and the body that there may be something dangerous here, but he is not quite sure.

When we perceive a threat, the threat can be external, such as an event with lots of people, making a decision about important future plans, paying at the till in Sainsburys or teenage daughter going to her first house party.

Or the threat can be internal, remembering distressing childhood events, thinking about all the things in life that need our attention, or the responsibility of a job, child, marriage.

Don't forget the amygdala is thousands of years old and is not really up to date with what is dangerous and what's not.

IF AT THIS POINT, IF WE CAN'T MANAGE TO DISTRACT OR DAMPEN THAT FEELING WITH TECHNIQUES SUCH AS SELF TALK, GROUNDING etc. THEN THIS HAPPENS.

1. The BOSS (prefrontal cortex) part of the brain goes out to lunch, logic, reasoning, problem solving, directing attention is now much harder to access.

2. The Security Guard wants to check with the BOSS if there is a real danger, but the BOSS has gone, so there is no rational thinking left and the security guard decides to do the next best thing.

3.   He goes to the Secretary (hippocampus) and gets her to check her "files" (short term and long-term memory) She is also feeling the pressure and quickly sends back the memories that vaguely match the perceived threat.

4.   The Security Guard, who is a bit enthusiastic, has been told above all else 'keep them safe and alive' so being safe rather than sorry is the best way to go. The security guard floods the system with adrenalin in preparation for fight or flight, the problem becomes that there is no fight or flight situation and that energy does not get discharged.

All this happening over a long period of time floods the brain with cortisol. If this is chronic and sustained, this can have a lasting effect on the creation of new memories and accessing existing ones.

What about the physical symptoms then?? There must be some sort of threat for me to feel that terrible while I am anxious?

If the brain can't determine real threat under pressure then the body certainly can't, the brain is running the show, so it sends lots of physiological helpful procedures to the body.

Your heart pounds to send oxygen to your muscles that are supercharged and ready. There is no need for the immune system and the digestive system, so this shuts down and we no longer feel hungry, this allows an extra bit of power for processing information in the brain.

Hearing becomes sensitized to detect every sound for survival; the pupils dilate to allow for more light and sharper vision.

There are two theories on why we sweat when anxious, one is too cool down and the other to make us slippery and more difficult to grab hold of in the hunt.

As you can see, all these responses are geared up for the hunter gather who existed years ago. These responses aren't needed in the majority of anxiety provoking situations but the amygdala can't determine this. I was going to cover maintaining factors in anxiety this week, but I believe it is best to digest this information, so when we feel anxiety it's easier to imagine that this process/response is happening. You can also explain to this process to your teenager easier now.

Anxiety lesson 3 Maintaining aspects of anxiety

Anxiety lesson 3

Avoidance is a major player in the maintenance of anxiety, avoiding an activity or object (external stimulus) or an image, memory (internal stimulus) will ensure your anxiety remains firmly in place. Avoidance feels good because it gives us a major feeling of relief, you don't have to tolerate the terrible anxious state. All the time we do this though we are hardwiring our anxiety.

A less extreme version of avoidance is to face the anxiety provoking situation, but to employ safety behaviours, these are things we do that allow us to get through the situation (some people would describe it as endure the situation) When people suffer acute paralysing anxiety they describe living as just surviving. If you think about safety behaviours as shields that prevent new learning taking place, for example:

·   Sit on the edge of a group, not really interacting and hoping you won't be noticed.

·   Taking the children to an event where you would feel anxiety so you won't be able to experience panic and face the fear, as you have to keep it together and they are a distraction.

· Don't ask questions and avoid talking about yourself.

· Avoid situations where you are assessed on a formal level, driving test, fundraising for the PTA, not putting yourself forward for a promotion.

Self-talk/beliefs

The things we say to ourselves are rocket fuel for anxiety, they can come from comparisons with other people, "she's cleverer, smarter, stronger, funnier, successful, organised"

MOST OF ANXIETY IS ABOUT THINKING WE WONT COPE, but when do we ever think in detail about what not coping would look like and what practical steps we would take in that situation.

Withheld feelings

This creates base line anxiety and comes from feelings of frustration, sadness, shame, Anger. My clients who suffer with social anxiety usually have unexpressed anger from a time when they felt powerless in an episode of exclusion, isolation, suppression, ridicule. We can feel angry at other people but believe if we express this and show that side of us then we will be further rejected and so the cycle continues. Unexpressed anger manifests as anxiety.

Lack of assertiveness

This is similar to the above, lack of assertiveness breeds resentment. What happens is that you are accommodating, you don't state your need or point of view and you end up being put upon and overlooked this is turn makes you feel overwhelmed which causes anxiety.

Teenagers can suffer with this in terms of being the emotional rock for friends or being the one who takes on more in the group activity. It can also happen with parents when the teenager can't express a want or need due to parent's ill health/fragile state etc.

Coping capacity

When we have experienced anxiety for years and feel we have just about managed to get through life presenting a different self, we start to believe that we haven't got any real coping capacity. if something truly terrible were to happen to us or our families then we would be convinced that we don't have the strength, strategies, resolve and experience to get through it. Christine Padesky who is a leader in her field of Cognitive behaviour therapy talks about developing an assertive defence of self to reduce anxiety. This is where you practice facing challenging statements in the therapy room, learning how to be assertive and resilient for the outside world. This is something we will discuss later in the series.

Meaningful purpose

Sometimes when we don't have a meaningful purpose that gives us focus and energy, we become frustrated and agitated, we perceive that we are trapped, leading to sense of boredom and dissatisfaction, this along with high stress factors such as children with additional needs, difficult family dynamics, repetitive work, lead to anxiety being experienced.

In the case of teenagers, I have noticed that if my clients don't feel a sense of creativity in their lives where they can escape from the high stress of GCSE's, family dynamics and friendship issues, life start to feel like a daily grind from a very young age.

A note on social media and anxiety

We were not built to sit around all day with flickering eyes watching one video after the next. Our bodies were created for movement whether that be running to hunt down an animal or movement through music or competitive sports. I have worked with lots of teenagers to reduce their screen time and incorporate more movement into their daily lives and they always report their anxiety lessening as a result. There are lots of ways to incorporate it, not just running or family walks, I will discuss this further into the series of blogs.

Take a quick look below and consider what factors may be maintaining your anxiety

- Avoidance of phobic situations

- Negative self-talk, anticipating bad outcomes

- Mistaken beliefs about ourselves and other people

- Withheld/denied feelings

- Lack of assertiveness and belief in lowered coping capacity

- Lack Meaningful purpose

- Ruminating which backs up the anxiety from the back end maintains anxiety, you recall distressing experiences over again, trying to work out how you could have made it different. You link these together and form a storyline that reinforces a core belief "it was always going to go wrong, I'm crap at being a leader, girlfriend, friend"

So how can I work on one thing this week, I hear you say?

Well ruminating about the perceived failures reinforces the belief in lowered coping capacity. Most people have a collection of good and bad episodes, some have lasted months others are a singular thing you have said or done that you wish you hadn't.

In order for you to start to build the notion that you are 'capable and strong', you will need to take some time in the day where you consciously think about the things that have gone right, the situations you managed well.

PLEASE NOTE: THIS IS NOT THE SAME AS CHANGING NEGATIVE SELF TALK IN THE MOMENT, THIS WILL STILL CONTINUE... we will come onto that at a later stage.

This involves thinking of your challenges as survival and strength, not in terms of defeat, because you didn't handle X, Y and Z right.

So, I am going to give you some of my examples, please note I have to practice this every day, it is like a mental muscle that grows stronger with exercise.

· I found help for my son when I realised there was a developmental problem. As a result, he received portage services, speech and language therapy and the correct monitoring from children paediatrician services.

· I didn't pass the grammar test like my three older siblings, but I developed a strong sense of empathy and understanding for the people that have got more to offer than academia.

· The teachers picked up on my hearing impairment when I was 8, I was behind in my learning but I had developed a skill in creative poetry and pottery alongside this. I also developed a strong love of reading in this time, that has continued to bring me great comfort, it also informs my writing, or should I say gives me the confidence to write.

· I had a turbulent and abusive relationship in my 20's, but it taught me what I didn't want and gave me a strength to move through things instead of around them.

· My dad died when I was 14, it was incredibly sad for a long time. It taught me that things don't stay crap forever. We miss him as a family every day, he was so unique and larger than life. However, I now have a step dad who is equally encouraging, calm, considered and positive in his approach. Asking why is ok for a little while, but after a time it attracts more negative emotions and prevents you from dealing with other more important emotions.

Okay, so the flip negative side of these is:

·   Why does it have to be my son that struggles and needs all these services?

·   Why couldn't I go to grammar, like the others? I am stupid and being clever really matters. It was the exam pressure, I'm no good with exams.

·   Why did I have to catch up on that work, I wish I didn't sit at the front of the class. I wish I had been up to speed and I would have done something with my life MUCH sooner. I would be 'successful'.

·   Why was he abusive? It was about me and my reactions to things. I wish I didn't have to go through that. I shouldn't have had to go through that.

·   I made that bad choice of a boyfriend because my dad died. Everything leads back to dad dying. People who lose a parent during teenager years really suffer. What is the positives about someone dying? People think they have it tough, but they have both of their parents.

Here is a little insight for you. THIS IS NOT EASY!! It takes practice. Some of you may do meditation or running or emptying the dishwasher (if you've got your teenager to complete this task spontaneously, please get in contact to advise how) Then you have the time every day to complete this homework. This really matters because all the time it is reinforcing the failure thinking. Let's get on top of this... and then move through the maintaining causes/habits going forward.

It is important that you do not do this in a 'everything is positive, nothing is tough' kind of way. That isn't what this is about, we are accepting that it was crap/tough/distressing ect, but we are choosing to focus on what it gave us, so that we can be on top of things when it doesn't feel like we are.

For teenagers to do this, it is a bit tougher because they have less years of life experience, but it's still possible.

If you as a teenager would like some practice at this... or as a parent you think your teenager may benefit, then please go to Talking to Teenagers on Facebook and leave a comment on the original post. I will do a live video with teenagers using your profile (mum or dad) if they do not have one of their own and we will do a lesson on this to get you started.

Anxiety lesson 4 -Get on top of these 3 things before we tackle the self-talk.

I'm going to say something conversional now, I will get comments and dislikes. People may question whether I know my stuff, but the simple fact is, in my opinion, mindfulness is not an effective enough therapeutic intervention for children and adolescents. The therapeutic benefit of mindfulness is hard to dispute…for adults. It is great for the people that have practised it and managed to maintain it in everyday life, but I see a lot of young people that say it's hard to get used to and doesn't work.

It doesn't help that mindfulness has been sold as a 'treatment' for anxiety, you're going to become the non-anxious and chilled person you see on travel adverts. The truth is that you will be able to 'manage' your anxiety with this practice.

Mindfulness is being in the present moment, paying attention with the senses to the present thing we are experiencing. It is calming and restorative, but it takes practice and feels very opposite to the churning bodily responses we have when experiencing anxiety. I was doubtful that this intervention was the right one for children and teenagers before I heard reports from my clients that they didn't find it effective. I was absolutely certain that school was not the place to expect young minds to adopt it on mass.

A report by the Campbell Collaboration which can be read here
https://www.thetimes.co.uk/article/mindfulness-lessons-can-harmchildren-6n82276vs

Suggests that

Children and adolescents may not be developmentally ready for the complex cognitive tasks, focus and level of awareness that mindfulness-based interventions require," it added.

The analysis, by four academics, reviewed 61 studies of mindfulness in North America, Asia and Europe. It concluded: "We know little about the costs and adverse effects of school-based mindfulness interventions. The costs of implementing these programmes may not be justified and there are some indications that mindfulness-based interventions may have some adverse effects on children and youth — however, these have not been adequately examined."

The article below argues the case for not using mindfulness with traumatised clients, which begs the question... how is it possible for school staff to detect and understand which ones of their pupils have experienced developmental trauma? In simple terms, they can't know with any certainty.

http://upliftconnect.com/mindfulness-when-not-to-use-it/

So, I thought it may be worth discussing in this blog the very concrete things we could do to help reduce our anxiety intensity level, before we try and adopt the harder things mentioned in last week's blog. Ask your teenager to read and follow these things to take the edge off their anxiety. These are the first things I address with my teenage clients when they are suffering with increasing anxiety.

Sleep – I have written about this in an individual blog here, take a read, the statistics are unsettling

https://helenharveycounselling.blogspot.com/2017/08/lets-talk-about-sleep-teenagers-and.html

The essence of the blog is that lack of sleep contributes to poor mental health in a big way, it increases our feeling of sadness and anxiety. So how can teenagers get better sleep?

· Bath 1 hour before bed

· Read Harry Potter or similar book that your teenager used to love but is now "not cool". Could be read for half an hour, this brings comfort.

· Last digital interaction an hour and a half before planned sleep time

· No phones, tablets, ticking clocks or tv in the bedroom

· No performing difficult mental work before bedtime

· No watching the news (more on this later)

· If your teenager naps at the weekend NO MORE THAN 40 mins (anything more is disrupting your sleep pattern)

· If they experience waking in the night, then they can listen on audiobook (no phones… so needs to be cd Walkman) something like Wind in the Willows or Danny the Champion of the World. Simple stories that involve nature with nature sounds.

Being less informed – Tune out to the daily news.

Do you need to know how it feels to smell burning flesh from a volcano disaster in Indonesia? Told to you by Kay Burley and her outside broadcast reporter in great detail from sky news...no!

Do you need to know the incredibly sad detail of a father punched outside a night club who later died and what sad messages have been left on the flowers...no!

I could go on, but I don't need to because you can empathise with it, just by knowing about it. Nothing they will report will prepare you in case it happens to you. Its sensationalist and high drama and it is now piped out 24 hours a day... do your anxiety a favour and tell yourself and other people that you don't tune into the news. If bird flu strikes, be rest assured someone will mention it to you before you notice the empty poultry shelves in Tesco.

Exercise- I nearly dare not mention this one, as people suffering with anxiety get tired of hearing about exercise and endorphins, but it is about more than endorphins, it is about expelling the excess adrenalin being dumped into your body by the fight or flight response you get with anxiety. Teenagers can get exercise in all sorts of ways.

· Biking to friends

· Walking to the shop to get you some milk

· Hoovering the car (a bribe will be required from parents)

· Teaching younger siblings to play cricket, rounders, pogo stick (a bribe will be required from parents)

· Going on the scooter

- A walk to go geocaching (it a worldwide treasure hunt that is internet interactive which you can get on your phone for coordinates)

Put simply... do less exercise and your mood will decline, your anxiety will rise, you will feel less in the mood to exercise and more like a jittery sparrow who jumps when the phone rings.

It is interesting to note that outdoor swimming helps with anxiety as immersing ourselves in cold water more than four times acclimatises our stress response in different situations and seems to make our anxiety symptoms more manageable. It also tires the body naturally which aids sleep. I can personally vouch for this. I swim 10 months out of 12 in a wetsuit and it manages my mood and contributes to my wellbeing. It is just the BEST feeling! Work on these this week and then we will address the self-talk on next week's blog.

If you have found this blog informative, please subscribe, like and share the original post on Facebook.

The above things are some of the content of a first session, that is absolutely important to discuss before we work on negative self-talk, mistaken beliefs etc.

Anxiety lesson 5 - Negative thinking and self-talk

Do you feel like you are putting on a mask when you have all this anxiety and you don't want the world to know? Do you have constant negative chatter going on?

We assume that situations and not cognitions (your judgement of threat) is responsible for your anxiety. Anxious and fearful people are much more likely to overestimate the intensity of threat, which of course then leads to avoidance of situations. We do this by reinforcing the negative all the time with negative thoughts and self-talk.

Negative thoughts and self-talk is automatic, we have hundreds of negative thoughts every day and catching them as they run through your brain and looking at them closer is a very difficult thing indeed and takes a lot of practice. YOU CAN LEARN TO SLOW DOWN AND NOTICE YOUR NEGATIVE TALK

With self-talk comes a whole host of other information that is lumped together such as images, memories and associations. Identifying self-talk may be about unpicking several thoughts from an image or single word.

Also, the negative talk or thought is almost always irrational, it sounds so convincing and truthful that it is hard to ignore. It really does become the truth because the anxious state doesn't allow for us to consider information that it contra to that thought.

Negative self-talk/thoughts reinforce avoidance. You talk to yourself let's say about the bus being dangerous 'people stare at me when I get on'

'I won't get my words out when buying a ticket and the bus driver will be annoyed'

'the last time I got on the bus it didn't feel safe'

'there are always people that want to make conversation on the bus and I can't make conversation'

So, you avoid getting on the bus and will employ any strategy that helps you to avoid getting on the bus. The bus becomes this terribly awful thing that is no longer about buying a ticket and just sitting down until it's time to get off, instead it is an event that involves the very worst-case scenario on the bus journey from hell. In short, anxious thoughts leads to avoidance of the situation it also stops us considering the most likely outcome.

Self-talk can start or heighten a panic attack and although I don't want to concentrate on panic attacks in this blog, it is worth explaining that self-talk at the beginnings of a panic attack starts to turn all our focus inward. At this point we no longer notice what is happening around us, we just focus on our psychological feelings

E.g. *"My heart is pounding faster"*

"I feel dizzy"

"what if I collapse"

"I've gone hot and my chest has gone tight, that's the start of a heart attack"

So, the fear of this exacerbates the symptoms, without wanting to sound unkind. It becomes a self-induced state. From now on name it 'false panic talk' More on panic attacks later in the blog series.

Anxious Negative self-talk always assumes the worst. 'Everybody has done more revision than me, I'm going to fail'

To counter this thought you would say

1) "*you can't work on what everyone else is doing, you can only work on what you are doing. 2) A more real statement would be 'Some people will have done more revision than me, some will have done about the same and some will have done less'*"

3) "*Where is the evidence that people have done more revision*".

4) "*Historically how many exams have I totally failed (this requires you to mentally go back one by one and literally tick them off)*"

5) "*I am confident I have done all I can, let's see how it goes*"

"*My future mother in law is coming, I have to make sure everything is perfect. She has to like me*"

To counter this thought you would say

"*why wouldn't she like me, I'm a good person*"

"*is it actually true she has to like me, is it necessary for my wellbeing that she approves of me*"

What is the worst that could happen, I am surviving and have other people who care for and support me"?

When you counter the anxiety self-talk, it must be in the present tense because the negative self-talk it in the present tense. E.g. "I am confident, I am surviving"

So, the questions are:

What is the evidence that supports this, if I took this thought to court could I prove it was true?

Am I basing this thought on facts or on feelings?

Is it an all or nothing thought? (the more likely scenario is always in between)

If my friend said this to me how would I respond?

It is hard to do at first, I have attached a thought sheet so you can record your thoughts and work on them.
https://www.therapistaid.com/worksheets/socratic-questioning.pdf

It is a whole new habit to create, but we create habits all the time that sometimes aren't good for us. This does require work, maybe it could be a new year's resolution to work on negative self-talk and with this will come self-compassion. This can only be positive.

Anxiety lesson 6 – Expression of feelings

It's not uncommon for people with anxiety disorders to withhold their true feelings. There are many reasons for this, one common one is the need to be in control and a fear of losing it. When feelings have been denied over time, anxiety can start to manifest. I wrote about this briefly in Anxiety lesson 1 potential causes
https://helenharveycounselling.blogspot.com/2017/10/anxiety-learning-potential-causes.html

Because people with anxiety/phobic tendency tend to be emotionally hastier and have very strong feelings, the expression of them is even more important for their emotional well-being.

When I did my degree in Person Centred Therapy, it was a requirement that you checked in with yourself and others in the morning, also a portion of the day was dedicated to personal development. Again, this is a discipline that requires practice, to notice and name feelings and the memories/events that are contributing to them. Sometimes this stuff sits on our edge of awareness (meaning we have a sense of it, but not a concrete image or thought)

The blob tree can be a useful introductory resource for identifying feelings, some colleges use these with their students, but not in the right way as they don't give the student enough time to explore why the student identifies with that particular blob. It works well with young people as it is visual and simple in its presentation. It is worth noting that we used it in a therapeutic community for substance misuse where residents (before they came into treatment) had spent a lifetime denying and hiding feelings through alcohol and drugs. It worked for them as a gateway to start to communicate feelings. You can access it here and print it off. Pip Wilson's work is genius and there are lots of different versions of blob trees.

The Blob Tree

http://www.pipwilson.com/p/blob-tree.html

Every feeling we have holds a charge of energy, when we do not give expression to it, there is a tension that exists. Some school of therapies believe that depression is anger turned in against the self. It may be worth exploring if you feel remaining anger from earlier periods of your life. Loss and disappointment sometimes contribute to anxiety, the loss may not be somebody, but a goal, status, position, loss of trust etc.

We need to ask ourselves "where in the body does this feeling live", if we cannot get the right word for it then please refer to this PDF document of feelings here
https://www.cnvc.org/sites/default/files/feelings_inventory_o.pdf

Individuals who are prone to anxiety are sometimes people pleasers, they are unable to express their true views and feelings for fear of appearing angry or oppositional, these trapped feelings and the need to express them manifest as anxiety.

Before you express your feelings to someone, you need to be able to express them in the right way to ensure you are understood and emotionally held.

"I" statements are the first place to start. "I'm feeling" or "I feel" not

"you make me feel" expressing feelings this way means you own them.

If you are trying to express how you feel due to someone else's treatment then it is going to go smoother if you say "when you say blah blah, I feel as if" or "When you do blah blah, I'm afraid I will be left on my own."

Think about what messages you received as a child about expressing anger

Does it feel ok for you to feel angry?

Are you being aggressive/assertive/stubborn/complaining

Think about what messages you received as a child about sadness and loss

Does it feel ok to feel sad?

What messages were you given as a child about crying? Where you afraid you were burdening an already overwhelmed parent?

Do you feel relieved or ashamed about crying, I am weak etc.

Writing a letter communicates feelings (whether sending it or not) and you can do this in conjunction with the blob tree. You can enter these into a nice scrap book with the corresponding blob and it becomes a journal of feelings. This is the first step in recognising and acknowledging unprocessed/unexpressed feelings. Once you have got used to recognising the feelings and acknowledging then you are better able to communicate them to another person.

For adults communicating feelings to our parents is a tricky business.

Anxiety lesson 7 – lets evaluate our positive beliefs about worry

This is going to be a short blog and I would like you to print this off and stick it to the fridge.

When anxiety and worry have existed for some time, we develop positive beliefs about this awful paralysing condition. These beliefs are sometimes the following:

1) Worry helps me find solutions to my problems

2) Worrying is a motivator and so it means I get things done

3) Worry is a protective factor from negative things happening, should negative things happen then I will be prepared.

4) Worry can prevent negative things from happening (miracle thinking, thought action connection) 'If I worry about this strongly enough, it won't happen'

5) Worrying about people and situation means I am a caring and compassionate person.

That's address these individually

1) Do you actually solve your problems by worrying about them, do you come up with solutions after endless sessions of worry? Or does the problem just go around and round without structured problem solving. The worrying makes you anxious so that the prefrontal cortex area is off line and you can then not access rational, logical problem-solving thought.

2) Can you think of successful, motivated people who are not worriers? I want you to take a pen and paper and write down the people, how active they are in getting things done and if

they are successful. Are you confusing worrying with caring, you can care that you get things done, that the children are ok, that you are successful at your job/school, but you don't have to worry about it all the time. Does worry really improve your performance in any aspect of life or does it make you unable to concentrate, tired, memory problems.

3) There must be things that you worried about beforehand and then they happened, did it lessen the pain or impact on you. Where you protected from the sadness because you had worried about it. Worrying increases the negative emotions in the here and now.

4) This means that worry in itself enhances the prevention of negative outcomes. **So, if you reverse this and really really wish you could win the lottery and think about winning the lottery all the time, does that increase the probability of winning the lottery...NO**

5) Is there anything else you do that shows you are caring and conscientious, think of other people you consider caring and conscientious, that don't worry. What are their positive attributes that make them that way, are they similar to yours?

Think about the impact that excessive worry has had on your relationships, such as partner, children, sibling relationships. Do your teenagers believe you to be intrusive, or for young people, do your friends say your worry is excessive and no fun.

Worrying is a passive stance, finding solutions is an active stance. This blog is about unravelling positive beliefs about long standing worry. You are not going to change those positive beliefs straight away. However, you need to change your thinking and consider how much time has been spent worrying about hypothetical things that didn't happen. How uptight you have felt and for how long.

It's a bit like giving up drinking or smoking, you need to think about how it damages you now, how it no longer serves you and then think about all the time you could gain from not excessively worrying.

You have to believe in the cause before you can carry out the action. Print this out and stick it on your fridge. I will include the original word document for easier printing.

Anxiety lesson 8

Asserting yourself

Assertive behaviour helps control anxiety levels, it reduces feelings of emotional and everyday overwhelm. To be assertive you need self-awareness, you need to figure out what worries you, be able to recognise mounting stress, be able to recognise the feeling of being overwhelmed. When you have become quite good at this you have to practice treating yourself as you would a friend or a relative that you look after. If a friend or relative was being put upon, I am guessing you would eagerly stand up for their right to make their own decision and exercise their own autonomy. This is something that is required for you to become assertive.

On top of this knowledge you will need to practice the belief that you have a right to ask for what you want and have a boundary of what is acceptable behaviour (from others) in your life.

For young people this is tricky because for adult's, their life experience and the feelings that it leaves us with, is an indicator to what we don't want in our lives. Saying this, I have worked with plenty of young people that have been able to understand and except why someone would treat them a certain way, but also not put up with that behaviour and except it.

Let's look at what non-assertive behaviour looks like.

<u>Non-assertive behaviour</u> is when is when you agree to something to meet somebody else's wants and needs while ignoring your rights and needs. If you do give people the message that you are not certain you have the right to make a decision in your best interests or don't have the right to meet your own needs, other people will most likely ignore your uncertain stance and push for

their needs. This non-assertive communication is usually a want to be pleasing and liked by everyone, but soon leads feelings to overwhelm.

Aggressive behaviour (which some people mistake as assertive) is self-centred and unpleasant, I would like to say that aggressive communication is easy to notice, but it isn't (not the same as passive-aggressive). You would need to look out for a raising of the voice and what it physically does to your heartbeat and tummy in the moment. Sometimes it starts with

"Are you saying that"

"Are you trying to say"

"I can't believe, I feel insulted"

Aggressive communication is insensitive and the resulting feeling is of being wounded and emotionally hurt.

Passive aggressive communication

Passive aggressive communication is not confronting the issue with an honest conversation, but instead it is something like this

"well I can put it to the other staff, but I can't imagine they will be pleased, I can't guarantee what their actions will be" (threatening)

For teenagers their response is usually a mixture of half angry/sulky/guilt inducing. E.g. *"yeah it upset me a little bit, why wouldn't it, I'm not sure I can come to the birthday meal on Saturday now, mum says I need to do more stuff I enjoy with my other friends"* this can be said to someone in person, but with teenagers it is usually text or message. (notice it communicates sulky, threat of isolation and disapproval)

Long pauses in conversation also are sometimes a way for somebody to be passive aggressive. It indicates disagreement, but also makes you feel uncomfortable.

So, what does assertive behaviour look like?

It is asking for what you want without apologising. Responding to requests with an honest answer in a direct way. It is honouring your wants and needs, knowing you are allowed to do this. In a nut shell it is about meeting your own needs whilst respecting the other through direct communication. People like the directness of it, they know where they stand.

So, at the beginning of this blog I spoke about self-awareness and knowing what worries you and what you feel in relation to other people.

It might be helpful to think about which people you are non-assertive with, here are some suggestions

Parents

Fellow workers

School friends

Old friends

Spouse

Employer

Mother in law

Sales people, clerks, hired help

Now think about when you behave non-assertively.

Stating a difference of opinion

Expressing feelings

Saying no

Voicing when something annoys you

When someone criticises you

Making requests

Suggesting an idea

Dealing with people who try and make you feel guilty

Making a complaint

You could rate the above in degrees of discomfort and next week we will be discussing how we can become more assertive, including non-verbal behaviour, recognising your rights, learning assertive responses. And information on how you can role play this in your spare time.

Not a sales pitch but for people who are experiencing non-assertive behaviour in the work place, if you would like some help and strategies to make your working environment more pleasant. Please contact Ruth at www.theconsultcentre.com with over 22 years of business management and assertiveness training, she can help you feel more assertive in every area of your life.

Anxiety lesson 9 - What is assertiveness and Assertive communication?

When we think about assertiveness what springs to mind is often the thoughts, feeling and concern we have when we imagine having to stand up to others, challenge an opinion or to speak up. How we feel about being assertive is often a reflection of how much we are affected by it. Whether we are affected by it because we have been on the receiving end of assertiveness or because we are afraid of being assertive ourselves, the anxiety is often the overriding feeling.

Why is that? Well we often have an experience we go to in our mind when we think about it and in most cases that memory is a negative one. It is a memory of being shouted at or of a loss of control.

And there is the misconception.

Being assertive is nothing to do with conflict, it is not a negative experience. I would go so far as to say that when people think that being assertive is creating conflict, they could not be further from the truth.
If you have been on the receiving end of conflict, raised voices, shouting to gain attention, to lay down the law, to increase the

impact, if you consider it for a moment. Was it useful, did it bring around a lasting change in behaviour for you? Did it improve the relationship in a long-lasting way? I doubt it. And that is because conflict is a negative experience and it is not communication, and that is not being assertive.

Communication is a two-way process, a way in which two people can converse, relate and discuss.

Assertiveness in communication is no different. It is a conversation, a conversation where opinion is respected, challenge to views are given, but given constructively.

Your opinion is your own and nobody has the right to tell you otherwise. They do have the right to tell you they don't agree and you have the obligation to acknowledge that there can be different views on the same subject/situation or event.

Assertiveness is as much about listening as it is about talking. Communication is a healthy mix of listening and responding. Not waiting for the other to finish so that the opposing point can be given. So often in life, we don't listen to respond, instead we are waiting for the other to finish and are not responding to their statement, instead we just want to say what we think.

"The biggest communication problem is we do not listen to understand., We listen to reply." Stephen R. Covey

You can't control what others say, but you can control how you respond, and in essence that is what assertive communication is a test of, learning to respond positively to even the most hurtful of communication is as much about assertiveness as it is about confidence.

"I think you are lazy and you do nothing around the house, I am left with everything to clean up and I want your help now!" instead perhaps an assertive positive alternative could be *"I remember what it was like to be a teenager you know, and I know you think I nag, but right now I could do with your help, you are better than this, let's not be sat in our bedroom all day, I'd love you to come and spend some time with me, and let's get this done today"*

"you are such a kill joy, you never let me go with my mates, their mum's aren't like this, they are way cooler and they let them do what they want, I bloody hate this" a positive alternative *"look I know you think that I don't understand that you worry, but if I promise to ensure that I am safe, and that I am not hanging around, would you let me to go this once and let me prove to you that you can trust me?"*

Why Does It Matter?

An assertive communication style can help us do the things we want to do. But it goes further than that: Being assertive shows we respect ourselves and other people.

Some benefits in assertive communication are, you can give your opinion, you can ask for what you need, you can say NO and not feel guilty, you can speak up for yourself and for others.

People who speak assertively send the message that they believe in themselves. They're not too timid and they're not too pushy. They know that their feelings and ideas matter. They're confident.

How to be more assertive?

Here are some things you can try and they will get results

Start and consider what your style is, think of a situation in the past that has not gone well and think how you would have played this differently if you were being positively assertive

Pay attention to what you think, what you feel, and what you want to get from the interaction. You have to practice this, role play in it your head even before you do it in a real-life situation.

Think about how the other person may react, remember you aren't in control of that reaction, but you are in control of your next reaction to it.

Play out all the possible outcomes, have a response ready.

Look out for the words that come out of your mouth, if you are saying such things, as "I don't care" "It doesn't matter" "I don't know" and change these to "I would prefer" "I have thought about this and what I think is best for me is" "I feel what would be best for me is". And yes, this is about putting you first, about placing you in a confident stance.

Remind yourself that your ideas and opinions are as important as everyone else's. Knowing this helps you be assertive. Assertiveness starts with an inner attitude of valuing yourself as much as you value others.

Being less aggressive and changing to assertive

Let others speak first, as much as it may drive you mad – Let others speak "I would like to hear your thoughts on this" "I am keen to understand how you see the situation"

Don't interrupt, you have no idea how much courage it may have taken for the other person to speak, notice if you interrupt and say: "Oh, sorry — go ahead!" and let the other person finish
When you ask for an opinion listen to it! You don't have to agree, challenging is good, but don't dismiss "you are talking crap" is not a positive answer, but "You see I am having difficulty agreeing with you there and this is why"

Assertiveness should be harmonious not adversarial, remember it is not about who wins. It is about what is agreed.

· So, to clarify, you need to think about what your rights are in any given situation.

· Think about when is a good time to have a discussion with the person.

· Address the person and state the problem and the effects/consequences it has on you.

· Express your feelings about the situation.

· Make a request for it to change.

If you want to develop nonverbal assertive behaviours, look the person directly in the eye, looking sideways or down at the floor transmits the message that you are not sure of your stance. Maintain an open posture, no arms folded. The most difficult bit is the initial communication from you. Take a deep breath and say what needs to be said.

Learning to say no when you are put on the spot.

One of the most important aspects of being assertive is being able to say no to other people's requests. A firm '*No, I'm not interested*" or "*no thanks that is not my type of thing*", will suffice. If someone is asking you to do something practical for them you are allowed to say '*I'll give that some thought and let you know*', or '*let me think about that*', don't apologize for not knowing there and then.

You could write out an assertive response to each of your problem situations adding to them over the next three or four weeks. Once you have responded assertively two to three times and you feel a sense of relief and positive stance, you will want it to become a *way of being* for you.

This blog is brought to you by Ruth Wilkinson of https://www.facebook.com/LifeCoachLancashire/

Life coaching from a fully qualified, Master Coaching practitioner. No judgement, no pushing, advocate of your goals and providing belief in your potential

Anxiety lesson 10 – Just some pointers to lessen anxiety and bring a bit of stillness

- **Stagger life transitions, new job, new school for teenager and new partner is going to create anxiety. One thing at a time and make time just for one thing.**

- **Surround yourself with people who don't want something from you. Find people with an 80% positive outlook.**

- **Diary when your time of the month is and plan a self-care routine for the first 2 days of it.**

- **Say to yourself 'I feel quite calm actually' at frequent intervals. The positive drip drip of affirmations brings behaviour change.**

- **When you return home put your slippers on and a comfy jumper with your blanket on stand by for comfort**

- **Don't ruminate about past behaviour, people usually do this in a highly anxious state (front thinking brain cut off) it's pointless because you can't change what has happened and you're too anxious to learn from it to apply it the next time.**

- **Sort your kitchen and bedroom out, remove the clutter, you need the kitchen to function and your bedroom is your sanctuary, make it a pleasant space for wind down.**

- When interactions with certain people make you anxious, work out really quickly what this is about and if it is your emotional stuff or theirs.

- Concentrate on your own needs for 35 minute a day.

- If you can tolerate it, allow people to hug you, hold you, touch you. It is therapeutic. If you can't tolerate this go into nature and sit in the grass or on the beach or take your shoes off and walk on the ground.

- Actively ignore how much revision Sophie has done, or how much prep Jen has done on her presentation. You can't control what other people do, you can only control what you do.

- Turn the radio off in the car and have some quiet.

- Plan 15 minutes extra in for all tasks

- Sort your sleep out, look into ways to get better sleep. Be curious about sleep quality, google it and apply what you learn.

- Say 'I'll think about it' to more things while you work out what you want to say YES to.

- relax your body while walking, drop the shoulders, breath deep and slow your pace. Try doing it round the supermarket (its hard) but when you slow right down, you do feel calmer.

- Find what you are interested in and learn about it on the internet.

- Do something creative, drama, painting, dance, pottery, scrap book, photography

- Massage your feet, better still get someone else to do it.

- Have a plan, because if life feels scary then it's got to be better with a plan. It provides structure and minimises the unpredictability of events.

Ending

I hope you have found this short book informative. If you would like to keep up to date with Talking to Teenagers activity. Please join us on Facebook or twitter.

Printed in Great Britain
by Amazon